Detours

Tony Rickaby

Copyright © 2014 Tony Rickaby
All rights reserved.
ISBN-10: 1501019406
ISBN-13: 9781501019401

Tony Rickaby was born in 1944. He studied at Portsmouth College of Art and St. Martin's School of Art and has shown his conceptual works, installations and paintings throughout Europe and the US. His writings, poems and animations have appeared in a number of printed and online magazines. He lives in Brixton, London.

For Jack

Contents

Bomb Walk	1
Passage	8
Getting On	14
Station	23
Wee Willie Harris	26
Round the Estate	36
Footnotes '59	45
Art Outings	55
Can Man	65
Stockwell Road Shots	68
Corners	73
South Street	77
Martyrs' Days	87
To the River	102
Fitzrovia Junctures	108
Voyage	114
Leaving	117

Bomb Walk

I was conceived in a flat in this street. It must have been during my father's Christmas leave from the army. I was due to be born in the Royal Free Hospital in the Gray's Inn Road but, three months previously, a V1 flying bomb scored a direct hit on the building and so the expectant mothers were reassigned to other hospitals.

When walking, the body moves over the stiff leg with each step, only one foot at a time leaves contact with the ground and there is a moment when both feet support the body. A child is usually able to walk unassisted at around 11 months old.

Billy and Pauline go down the road and cross to the other side. I go after them. We get through the fence. The bombsite is good to play on. I've been told not to play here because it's dangerous. I might get into trouble.

In the afternoon of June 28 1944, a V1 flying bomb fell in Gauden Road, near Clapham North Tube station, killing 11 people. The previous night, just after midnight, a V1 fell farther up the road, killing one person. Two weeks later, at 3am on July 10, one hit Clapham Road. Four people were killed, six houses were demolished and 20 houses and a church severely damaged.

I finally find my phone and shut the front door behind me. Trying to get out of the house always takes too long. And once I do leave then I'll probably have to go back for something: credit card, or change or I should be wearing something warmer or to

make sure I've really locked the front door.
I'll walk. Should take about an hour.

Although walking speeds can vary greatly depending on such things as height, weight, age, terrain, load, culture, effort and fitness, the average is about three miles an hour.

On June 25 1944, just after midnight, a V1 bomb fell in Studley Road, demolishing 10 houses and severely damaging 30, including the Methodist church. Three people were killed. Two months later, on the afternoon of August 20, another V1 fell in Studley Road...

I cross over by the war memorial. Three men – they look Somali or Ethiopian – are getting out of a battered Fiat Punto. One is wearing a dark top with *NEW YORK* printed across the front.

'I think you'll get a ticket leaving it there,' I tell them, but they ignore me.

I'm talking to myself again. But only when I'm on my own, when there's nobody around. I know I'm doing it. Not whole conversations, just little questions like: 'Why can't that be true?' or 'How could that happen?' They often seem to be regrets for things in the past that I did or didn't do. Stupid things. Wondering how my life might have turned out if I'd made different decisions about certain things. I keep resolving to stop, but I can't help myself.

They get out of the car and stretch their arms in the air.
'Not sure we should park here,' says Ramzi.
Muktar shakes his head and looks at him with a strange expression on his face. 'Don't matter where you leave it now, does it? Think about it.'
'Why Stockwell anyway, man?' says Yassin. 'Why right down

south of the river? We could've chosen anywhere.'

'It was Hussain's idea,' says Ramzi. 'He lives in a flat round here. Well, his wife and kids do. He used to go to the mosque down the road there, but the imam wasn't a serious believer, so he stopped going.'

They gather round the boot of the car. Ramzi opens it up and Muktar lifts out three rucksacks, one after the other. 'Yeah, this'll be bigger and better than Mo's in July. You've got he purple one, Yassin.' He smiles. 'Okay with you?'

'Makes no difference to me, man. Where's the station from here?'

'Just up there round the corner,' Muktar points up the road and heaves his rucksack up onto his shoulders. 'Now...we're warriors, right? This is for the sake of Allah.'

'For he loves those who fight in his sake,' says Yassin.

Ramzi bangs the boot shut and they stand there gripping the shoulder straps of the rucksacks on their backs and leaning forward from their weight.

'So we're all clear, right?' says Muktar. Me and Ramzi get the Northern Line and you, Yassin, get the Victoria...and... we'll meet again...'

As I get to the top of Clapham Road, a man wearing a black top and white trousers runs very fast out of the Tube station and is chased across the road by a group of shouting people. The station flower seller drops a bunch of flowers and joins in.

'Stop! Stop him!'

But he's too fast for any of them.

He looked familiar.

During World War II, trench shelters were built in London's parks. The one in Kennington Park followed the standard design: two trenches joined by four shorter ones at right angles to them, making a closed grid each section of which could accommodate up to 50 people. The earth walls were reinforced with sandbags and the corrugated iron roof covered with a layer of soil. All trench shelters were prone to flooding and subsidence, so they were lined with thin concrete slabs. This 'ladder' design was dangerous: a direct hit would cause a collapse of the whole shelter and a bomb falling inside the grid between the trenches would create a shock wave sufficient to crush the trenches.

Some of these shelters had a zigzag design which could far better withstand the stresses of a direct hit, but the expense and lack of manpower made such a design for the Kennington Park trench impractical.

On October 15 1940, a 50lb bomb fell on the Kennington Park trench shelter. No official death toll was announced at the time but it was believed to be 104 fatalities. With the shelter walls collapsing due to the wet ground, rescuers digging the bodies out could eventually do no more and they covered the remains with lime. Most of the 48 recovered bodies were buried in Lambeth Cemetery. The rest still lie, unidentified, beneath the park.

I turn into Harleyford Street where there's a crowd, mostly of women, staring up at a parachutist floating down from the sky.

'He's a Jerry,' a smiling old man tells me, folding his arms. 'The bombing bastard.'

There are angry shouts as the crowd gets bigger. People run out of the flats and others lean over their balconies.

The German's parachute catches on a telegraph pole and he dangles there a few feet from the ground. Two women jump up and hit at him with umbrellas. Some throw stones, bits of wood. Others grab his legs, trying to pull him down as his blood drips onto them.

'They're after the parachute silk,' says the old man.

'Kamerad! Kamerad!' gasps the German.

They wrench him to the ground and kick and punch him as

he lays there, his face pale and bruised.

'I am an officer! I am an officer!'

'If they want that silk they'd better hurry – here come the coppers.'

The police push and drag the women away. 'Get away from him. Get away. We don't do lynching in this country.'

They kneel over the German, unbuckle his harness and the parachute is immediately snatched away. Four or five women pull it in different directions, yelling at each other as the police gently pick him up, carry him to their van, put him inside and drive off across the cricket ground. Suddenly embarrassed that I've been standing staring at all this, I move on.

Walking 30 to 60 minutes a day, five days a week, with the correct posture, reduces the chances of cancer, type 2 diabetes, heart disease, anxiety and depression. Life expectancy is also increased.

The pub that used to be run by my uncle and aunt isn't there any more. Neither is my uncle – he killed himself sitting in his car in Epping Forest with a hosepipe running from the exhaust in through the back window. In the same year they hauled the body of another uncle of mine out of the Thames. Both men had served in World War II.

This must be the place where I was told to meet up - behind the Vauxhall Tavern. I look at the poster outside: *Frank Sanazi's Blitz*. There's a park behind the pub, with the railway viaduct along one side and the arches underneath used for different things: *Metropolis Motorcycles, Chariots Roman Spa*. Is this the place? Gerry's not here and I'm starting to feel anxious.

On April 21 1749 there was a full rehearsal of *The Music for the Royal Fireworks* at Vauxhall Gardens. This suite, composed by George Frideric Handel, was commissioned by King George II to celebrate the end of the War of the Austrian Succession and the signing of the Treaty of Aix-la-Chapelle. Over twelve thousand people, each paying 2/6, tried to attend, causing a three-hour traffic jam of carriages after the main route to the Gardens was closed when the central arch of newly built London Bridge collapsed.

There's a tap on my shoulder and I jump. It's Gerry.
'Christ!... Don't do that.'
'Been here long? How d'you get here?'
'About five minutes – I walked.'
'I got the tube from Stockwell...So what now?'
'I guess we wait for him.'
Gerry lights up a cigarette and looks around. 'How long's he going to be?'
'Should be soon...Hang on – this is him.'
He's carrying a large canvas holdall over his shoulder. He shakes our hands.
'Right, are you two clear about what was decided at The Swan?'
We nod.
'Have you both got my number on your phones?'
We nod again.
'Okay,' he says to Gerry, 'you stay over there at the bus stop. If you see anything, any police, then ring me. When you hear the bang, disappear. And don't run.' He turns to me. 'You - follow me.'
'What bang?' I whisper. 'You never said anything about a bang.'
'Just come with me.'
I follow him through the deserted park until he stops at a small mound hidden by trees.
'Here's the spot.'
'What's going on?'
'You'll find out in a minute.' He kneels down, unzips the

holdall and pulls out a thick green tube.

'What the hell is that?'

'It's a Neto, an RPG 22. They're Russian. It can fire a rocket grenade right through a yard of concrete. We acquired some from a couple of lads who aren't too happy about the ceasefire. I think they got them from Yugoslavia.'

He slides out an extension to the tube then reaches into the holdall, pulls out a grenade and pushes it into the end of the tube. He flicks up the sights and hoists the launcher up onto his shoulder. 'Okay, all set.'

'What're you going to do with it for Christ's sake?'

'D'you see that big building over the railway line? You can just make out the lights of the top windows from here. Well that's the MI6 headquarters. We're going to give those bastards a fright.'

'You're going to fire that at the MI6 building? Over the railway? Jesus, d'you think you'll hit it?'

'Sure. Now, you get to the end of this road, where the park stops and, like I told your mate, if you see anything, ring me. And when you hear it go off, get lost.'

I walk quickly away and at the end of the road I stop and wait for a few minutes, gripping my phone. There's a flash then two bangs. I follow the road round the edge of the park and head south.

Passage

Francis swings backwards and forwards on the metal gate, listening to it squeaking. He looks back at the kitchen window and, when he sees that his mother isn't at the sink watching him, he pushes open the gate. He's frightened of going that way because of the big dog that barks and jumps up at the fence and might bite him. So he goes the other way and wanders along the narrow gravel path that runs between the backs of the prefabs, humming a tune he's made up.

His shadow on the ground is very black and he smiles at its funny shapes. When he kicks at the gravel, bits get in one of his sandals and he sits down to take it off, turn it upside down and put it back on again. Then he picks up something he sees lying on the ground. The dirt on it makes his fingers black so he throws the thing away, wipes his fingers on his shirt, stands up and continues along the path. Passing a hedge, he tries not to touch the cobwebs as he pulls off a leaf, bends it in half along the stalk, nibbles at the tip and spits out the green juice.

The noise of children laughing and talking comes from somewhere and when he turns the bend in the path he sees a girl and a boy standing against a wooden fence. The girl has curly hair and is wearing a blue dress and the ginger-haired boy wears long grey trousers with braces and a white short-sleeved shirt. Francis stops to stare at them and they stare back. 'What you doing?' he asks.

The girl, who is taller than the boy, pulls a face. 'We're playing,' she says.

'We always play here,' says the boy.

Francis smiles at them and puts his hands in his pockets. 'Can I play with you?'

They don't answer him.

'What you playing?'

'Games,' says the girl.

'What games?'

'Special games,' she says.

'What's that?'

'Special.'

Francis kicks at the ground. 'My name's Francis.'

The girl and boy laugh. 'That's silly,' she says. 'That's a girl's name.'

'No it's not.'

'Yes it is. What's your real name?'

'Francis Walsh.'

'Wishy washy!' the boy shouts.

Francis frowns at him. 'I can punch you if you call me that.'

The boy grins. 'We won't let you play with us then. But I can beat you up anyway.'

'What's your name?' asks Francis.

'Richard. And she's Christine.' He pushes a finger against the fence. 'We play in there.'

'What's in there?'

'Our secret place,' says Christine.

Francis puts his hand against the fence. 'What's a secret?'

'It's scary in there,' she says.

'Scary wary,' says Richard.

'We'll go to our secret place now,' says Christine. 'And play there.' She pushes open a slat in the fence. 'Come on.'

Richard, then Francis, follow her on hands and knees and squeeze through the gap in the fence into the corner of an allotment where Francis sees little sheds made of doors and bits of wood and rows of green things growing and hanging from big sticks.

'This is a funny place,' says Francis.

Christine puts a finger to her lips. 'You've got to be very quiet here and nobody must see you.'

'Ow!' says Francis when he catches his knee on a bramble.

'Shush!' she hisses.

With Christine leading the way, they creep through the long grass and tangle of weeds at the edge of the allotment. Richard turns to Francis. 'That's our den over there,' he says, pointing to some rusting sheets of corrugated iron leaning against the back of an old shed. They crawl underneath the sheets and sit down on the ground. Francis examines his knee, licks his fingers and wipes off the blood.

There's a brick on the ground and Richard pushes it over with his foot and screws up his face when woodlice and centipedes scuttle out. He picks a snail off the brick and holds it up to Francis's face. 'We can eat this when we get hungry.'

Francis shakes his head. 'No, I don't want to.'

'No one can see us here. We can be here for ever and ever,' says Richard as Christine reaches outside and picks up a few sticks and twigs.

'It's hot here. Do we play now?' asks Francis.

Richard points upwards. 'We're hiding from the bombs.'

'No, we're in hospital,' says Christine.

'What's that?' asks Francis.

'If you're sick.'

'From the bombs dropping on you?'

'From anything, silly.'

'Silly billy,' says Richard.

'Quiet,' says Christine. 'This is the hospital and I'm the doctor.'

Richard nods. 'I'm a doctor too.'

She shakes her head. 'No, you're the nurse.'

'That's silly,' he says. 'Girls can't be doctors and boys can't be nurses.'

'It's my game and I'm the doctor.'

'What will I be?' asks Francis.

'You're a patient.'

'What's a patient?'

'Somebody what's sick.'

'I don't want to be sick.'

'You must lie down and close your eyes because you're sick.'

'It's too dirty to lie down.'

'You can't play if you don't lie down.'

'All right.'

He lies down and Christine picks up a stick. 'We've got to examine you now.'

'What's that?'

'To see if you need medicine.'

She prods his stomach with the stick.

'That tickles.'

'It's a sick stick,' says Richard.

'You're very sick and you must have a jection.'

'No!'

Richard giggles. 'In the bum.'

'You have to take your trousers off.'

'I'm not sick. I don't want my trousers off.'

She frowns. 'I'm the doctor and you've got to do what I tell you. I've found out you might die and the jection will make you better. Nurse, take his trousers off.'

Francis looks at them both. 'Then can I be the doctor?'

'I'm the doctor.'

He slowly pushes down his khaki shorts. 'Eugh,' says Richard. 'They're dirty pants.'

'No they're not.'

Christine waves the stick. 'You've got to turn over for the jection.'

She pulls Francis over onto his side and he wriggles his body around as Richard pulls down his underpants. 'I don't like this game - it's rude.'

'You're a baby. Be quiet and keep still if you want to be

made better.'

When Francis stops moving, she turns to Richard. 'Nurse, give him a jection in here,' and Richard pokes a twig into his backside.

'Ow!'

'You'll be better now,' she says. 'You can put your clothes back on.'

Francis starts to pull up his pants and she points at his penis and laughs.

'You're rude,' he says, tugging up his trousers.

Richard starts laughing as well. 'This is a funny game.'

Francis sits up straight. 'Now can I be the doctor?'

'No, now you're the nurse. Richard is the doctor this time and I'm the patient. But I'm not lying down because it's too dirty.'

'You ject her this time,' says Richard, handing Francis a stick.

'Where?'

'On my belly button,' says Christine. She kneels on the ground, pushes down her navy blue knickers and lifts up her skirt with both hands.

Francis bends down and stares closely at her. 'You've got two belly buttons.'

'That one's her willy,' says Richard.

'It smells.'

'Yours smells,' she says. 'Yours is silly. It's small, not like my Daddy's.'

'Yours isn't there.'

Richard giggles.

'If you want,' she says, 'we can touch willies.'

'What for?'

'Mummies and daddies do it.'

Francis frowns. 'What for?'

'They just do.'

There's the sound of voices. Christine jerks up her knickers and drops her skirt and the three of them go very quiet.

'That's the men,' whispers Richard. 'They'll do things to you.'

Francis trembles. 'What things?'

'Nasty things.'

The corrugated sheet is pulled back and they blink at the sudden brightness. Francis jumps and gives a squeal. A man dressed in wellingtons and an old army jacket is staring down at them.

'I thought I heard something. What are you three up to?'

'This is our den,' says Richard.

'We're playing,' says Christine.

'Doctors and nurses,' says Francis.

The man grins and turns his head. 'Bill, come over here.'

Getting On

Calais is the heavily fortified command post for German forces in the Pas-de-Calais/Flanders region. The Germans believed that any Allied invasion would take place here, but when the D-Day invasion took place in Normandy, Calais was vulnerable to a land attack from the west. Eight days ago the town was bombed and shelled, followed by an assault by the 7th and 8th brigades of the 3rd Canadian Division with British and Canadian tank support that overwhelmed the garrison's 7,500 defenders. At 9 0'clock this morning, Calais, largely in ruins, surrenders.

She lies on the bed, naked from the waist down. Her knees are pushed up and wide open and a nurse stands either side of her. She rolls her head from side to side, her eyes are screwed tight, her teeth gritted together and her face is covered in sweat.

'Another deep breath,' says the nurse. 'And push...That's good – keep pushing. One, two, three, four, five, six, seven, eight, nine, ten. Push again. Harder.'

She wails and grips both of her knees as her head jerks backwards and forwards.

'Okay, now take a rest.'

She puts her head back on the pillow, panting and puffing out her cheeks.

'Right, another big push.' The nurse starts counting again.

'Aargh!' she screams.

'That's good – it's coming. Push long and hard.'

Another long scream.
'It's all done. All over.'

The Klever Reichswald, over 5,000 hectares in size, is the largest contiguous forest in the Lower Rhine. It lies southwest of Kleve in North Rhine-Westphalia in Germany between the Rivers Rhine and Maas at the Dutch/German border. Because the Reichswald is on a glacial ridge, it is not subjected to flooding, though the glacial gravel contains a lot of loam from the northern German plain and this causes the surface to become extremely muddy during a rainy period. The Battle of the Reichswald (code-named *Operation Veritable*) takes place between February 8 and March 11, 1945. This is part of the Allied push into Germany.

> Walkie round the garden
> Like a teddy bear.
> One step, two step,
> Tickle you under there!

He picks up the top of the Vicks jar, puts it in his mouth and swallows it. His uncle holds him upside down by one ankle and slaps him on his back until the top shoots out onto the floor. Then his mother helps him on with his brand new coat and tells him to go downstairs and wait for her outside. He stands on the pavement for a little while and then he hugs the lamppost and swings round and round it. When his mother appears she screams at him. The lamppost has just been painted green.

The aluminium Type B2 prefabricated house has an entrance hall, two bedrooms, a living room, hallway, fitted kitchen with hot and cold running water, cooker and built-in refrigerator and a fitted bathroom with a heated towel rail and a separate flushing toilet. The coal fire in the living room has a back boiler that heats water for the bathroom and kitchen and also provides ducted warm air for the bedrooms. Built-in wardrobes provide storage. It is decorated in magnolia, with gloss-green on all additional wood, including door trimmings and skirting boards.

He looks around the big cream-painted room. There are windows along one side and, on the wall opposite, a big round clock and photographs of the pope and the king. A blackboard nearly covers the far wall. The room is full of children sitting at wooden desks that are lined up in straight rows. Boys are on one side and girls on the other. They all turn and stare at him.

> 'Regulations made by the Minister shall impose upon local education authorities the duty of providing milk, meals and other refreshment for pupils in attendance at schools and county colleges maintained by them; and such regulations shall make provision as to the manner in which and the persons by whom the expense of providing such milk, meals or refreshment is to be defrayed, as to the facilities to be afforded (including any buildings or equipment to be provided) and as to the services to be rendered by managers governors and teachers with respect to the provision of such milk, meals or refreshment, and as to such other consequential matters as the Minister considers expedient, so, however, that such regulations shall not impose upon teachers at any school or college duties upon days on which the school or college is not open for instruction, or duties in respect of meals other than the supervision of pupils, and shall not require the managers or governors of a voluntary school to incur expenditure.'

A loud bell rings outside the classroom. 'It's milk time,' says the boy sitting next to him. 'And when we've drunk our milk it's playtime.'

'All of you, one by one, come up and take your bottle of milk and straw,' calls out the teacher. When it's his turn, he goes to the front of the class and picks out one of the small bottles of milk from the metal crate and a straw from a metal jug and goes back to his desk where the boy shows him how to push out the little slotted hole in the cardboard top of the bottle and stick the straw through. He sucks up half of the milk and then starts blowing, filling up the bottle with bubbles. The boy laughs and copies him.

> At the Ould Lammas Fair boys were you ever there
> Were you ever at the Fair In Ballycastle-O!
> Did you treat your Mary Ann
> To some Dulse and Yellow Man
> At the Ould Lammas Fair in Ballycastle-O!
> In Flanders' fields afar while resting from the War
> We drank Bon Sante to the Flemish lassies O!
> But the scene that haunts my memory is kissing Mary Ann
> Her pouting lips all sticky from eating Yellow Man
> As we passed the silver Margy and we strolled along the strand
> From the Ould Lammas Fair in Ballycastle-O!

He tells her that the capital of Iceland is Reykjavik, but the nun canes him on the hand when he spells 'their' as 'thier'.

> Soul of Christ, sanctify me.
> Body of Christ, heal me.
> Blood of Christ, drench me.
> Water from the side of Christ, wash me.
> Passion of Christ, strengthen me.
> Good Jesus, hear me.
> In Your wounds shelter me.
> From turning away keep me.

> From the evil one protect me.
> At the hour of my death call me.
> Into Your presence lead me,
> to praise You with all Your saints
> for ever and ever. Amen.

He is dressed in short white trousers, a white shirt buttoned up to the neck, white ankle socks and brown sandals. His hair is brushed neatly to one side. He holds new rosary beads and a new prayer book with a shiny cream plastic cover.

Kingy is a ball game in which those who are not 'He' have the ball thrown at them, without means of retaliation, and against ever-increasing odds. Anyone who is hit by the ball joins the He in trying to hit the rest of the players. Those who are throwing may not run with the ball in their hands but can pass the ball to each other. Those being thrown at may run and dodge as they like. The game continues until all but one has been hit and is 'out', and this player is declared 'King'.

> I was sick.
> And the gulls followed us
> all the way to
> Scotland wanting some
> tit-bits.
> I was sick.
> There is a garden
> fete.
> Been to a procession on
> Sunday.
> I've seen willie's moter-
> -bike.
> How is the wee fat pig.
> I get to school nice
> and early

Prince Monolulu is a horse-racing tipster and celebrity of the British racing scene. He became well-known after picking out the horse Spion Kop in the 1920 Derby, which came in at the long odds of 100-6, and from which he personally made £8,000. He is celebrated for his brightly coloured robes and feathered headdress which helps punters spot him in the racetrack crowds and for his cry 'I gotta horse!' sometimes alternating with 'Black man for luck!'. Although he claims to be a Jewish prince of the Falasha tribe of Abyssinia, his real name is Peter Carl Mackay, and he was born in the Caribbean island of St Croix in 1881. Monolulu frequently features in newsreel broadcasts, and he's probably the best-known black man in Britain.

They have been waiting a long time and he is very bored. His mother gives him money to get an ice cream and when he runs across the road to the shop he nearly bumps into a tall black man with feathers on his head and a long white coat who's walking down the middle of the street. The soldiers and sailors finally come and there are men wearing brass helmets and white gloves and riding horses.

> When I went to the circus.
> I saw a funny old clown.
> He went into the wall
> and comed Jumping out
> with a chair comeing out.
> Whith him, I saw the loins
> and the loin tamer.
> And there was a wizard
> on a tight rope

The Irish priest, Father Patrick Peyton, also known as the Rosary Priest, is the promoter of the 'Family Rosary Crusade' which aims to bind families together through their daily recitation of the rosary. His famous slogan is 'The family that prays together stays together'. The movement utilizes radio, films, outdoor advertising and television, and has had the help of Hollywood celebrities such as Bing Crosby, Ronald Reagan and Natalie Wood. In a 1946 radio broadcast he proclaimed: 'The rosary is the offensive weapon that will destroy Communism—the great evil that seeks to destroy the faith'. He has become best known for his series of mass rallies in major cities throughout the world and his visit to Britain this year has culminated in a rally at Wembley Stadium in London, attended by 85,000 people.

> Hail Mary, full of grace. The Lord is with thee.
> Blessed art thou amongst women,
> and blessed is the fruit of thy womb, Jesus.
> Holy Mary, Mother of God, pray for us sinners,
> now and at the hour of our death. Amen.

The first unrationed sweets go on sale today. Toffee apples are the biggest sellers, with sticks of nougat and liquorice strips also very popular. The Minister of Food has said that stocks are sufficient and he has ordered a one-off allocation of extra sugar to manufacturers to help them meet the anticipated surge in demand. Sugar itself, though, still remains rationed. The industry gives a warm welcome to the news. 'We are very glad about it,' says a spokesman for the Cocoa, Chocolate and Confectionery Alliance. 'We will do all we can to make it work.' Despite the heavy sales, there are no signs of panic buying, even though there are already shortages of the most popular brands.

> We are the boys and girls well known as
> Minors of the ABC
> And every Saturday all line up
> To see the films we like and shout aloud with glee.
> We like to laugh and have a singsong,

> Such a happy crowd are we.
> We're all pals together,
> We're minors of the **A – B – C!**

They run into the corner shop and jostle in front of the sweet counter, discussing and deciding. He chooses two Flying Saucers, a Sherbet Fountain, two Black Jacks and a gobstopper and pushes some money across the counter. The man puts the sweets into a white paper bag which he hands to him with sixpence change, just enough for Saturday morning pictures.

> Ten green bottles hanging on the wall,
> Ten green bottles hanging on the wall,
> And if one green bottle should accidentally fall,
> There'll be nine green bottles hanging on the wall.

He looks out the window at the houses and fields going past. He is happy and excited. The grown-up men are sitting at the back of the coach and they take dark brown bottles of beer out of the wooden crate and drink from them. His grandmother takes a bar of fruit and nut from her handbag and breaks off a square to give him. 'When will the singing start?' he asks her.

> 'To touch the hearts of your students and to inspire them with the Christian spirit is the greatest miracle you could perform, and the one that God asks of you, since this is the purpose of your work.'

The cream painted corridor has a high ceiling and gothic windows along one wall. His heart thumps, his stomach flutters and he feels as if he might wet himself. The door opens and a tall thin man in a black cassock, black skull cap and stiff white preaching bands stands there. 'Come in,' he says.

HOI! MISTER! YOU'VE LOST A £5 NOTE!
HE HASN'T SEEN IT!
BANG PHUT
YOU LITTLE SCAMP!
GOT IT!
HA! HA! HA!

In each of the sets of words given below there is one word meaning something rather different from the other three. Find the different word in each line and write it down:

a) alike, same, similar, somewhat.

b) pigeon, duck, goose, swan.

c) bus, conductor, passenger, driver.

d) this, that, the, those.

e) firm, rough, solid, hard.

f) desk, book, cupboard, drawer.

g) spade, earth, sand, gravel.

h) pretty, nice, charm, lovely.

i) justice, merciful, pitying, forgiving.

j) tumbler, cup, mug, jug.

k) fishing, rowing, climbing, swimming.

l) scarlet, blue, red, pink.

m) sewing, cotton, needle, calico.

The cruiser *Ordzhonikidze* brings Nikita Khrushchev and Nikolai Bulganin to Portsmouth. It is the first visit by the new Soviet leadership to a Western bloc country since Josef Stalin's death.

Belomorkanal is a cigarette made up of a hollow cardboard tube joined to a cigarette paper tube filled with tobacco. The hollow part of the tube is pinched to make two perpendicular flat surfaces, and this acts as a cigarette holder. Popular in the Soviet Bloc, it is one of the strongest cigarettes available.

Station

Someone's standing in front of me. He looks Ethiopian, or Somali. I think he's going to ask me for change, but he bends down, picks up a dog-end lying at my feet and walks away.

The steel wall of the shelter presses against my back. In places like this, where I have to hang around - bus stations, waiting rooms, supermarket queues, post offices - the only way I can cope is to either go into a trance or get obsessed with people: hating the way they speak so loud on their phones (is she talking to someone in Australia?) or wondering where they get their hair cut or why they wear clothes like that (isn't there a mirror in his house?). The time I've spent just waiting around must have added up to years. And what a fucking place this is - a wasteland of billboards and crazy architecture and shitty old tunnels under the railways lines and loads of traffic going round and round and spewing out fumes and buses never on time. Where's the bus? I could start to walk I suppose, but then what usually happens is that one comes along when I'm between stops and I miss it.

To my left, a woman wearing a blue anorak, turquoise trousers and with her hair pulled back in a bun is standing next to a man sitting down on one of the metal seats. He's unshaven, his eyes are dim, there's a large bump on the side of his head and clumps of his hair are missing. He's wearing khaki combat trousers, a red beret and a black coat that's falling off his shoulders. They must be from the hostel round the corner. She shakes his shoulder and he sways away, nearly falling off his seat. Holding a can in her hand, she limps away on tiptoes, stops, looks down at the pavement, picks up an old tube ticket and puts it in her pocket. He gets to his feet and shuffles over to a large black man leaning against the shelter window, says something and pushes him in the chest. The black man slaps him hard around his ear and he staggers back surprised. Then he holds out his hand but the black man refuses to shake it, so he walks away, smiling. I wonder whether I should have tried to step in, to explain that he was obviously out of it and didn't know what he was doing. But it's too late now and anyway, I'm too much of a coward.

I notice a woman coming out of the tube entrance. Is it her? Her face looks the same, but shorter hair and a different colour – darker. And she never wore clothes like that: leather coat, high heels. Thinner too – she looks pretty good. If it is her, what's she doing round here? She'd never come south of the river if she could help it. Perhaps she works nearby. Must be doing well – those clothes look expensive. Surely she's not working for MI6, not with her sort of politics. Unless she's changed in ten years – people do. It must be ten years or more. Ten years? Twelve? I'm no good at working out how long something's been.

Christ, that takes me back. Perhaps I should say hello. Should definitely say hello. But I don't know what she'd think about that - I look pretty rough at the moment. She might be pleased to see me or she could be embarrassed. But she's bound to remember me. Though you can never tell – some people are good about not remembering things and most women aren't very sentimental about the past. Well the ones I know aren't. I forget how long we were together – if you could call it together. It was always a bit on and off. But we had a few laughs and enjoyed ourselves. Perhaps I was a bit of a bastard sometimes – I don't know. Not that we ever lived together, she always preferred her flat. It was a terrible flat, but mine upstairs was worse. At least she tried to keep hers clean. And that bloke she went out with – he was weird. I can't remember what his job was, but he just used to appear and disappear. Sometimes he'd acknowledge you and other times pretend you didn't exist. One of those people who look over your shoulder when you're talking to them.

She'd be surprised to see me. Oh, she's off – in a hurry. I'll have to chase after her. Though I wouldn't want her to think that I'm following her or something. That would be a bit uncool. A bit creepy. Like a fucking stalker. Perhaps if I nip down one of those side streets and go round, double back and walk towards her, then I could make out I'm bumping into her by accident. But I don't really know where those streets go to. I'd probably get lost or something. I'm not even sure it's her.

Wee Willie Harris

I'm walking past a row of small shops. One of them was once a hairdresser's called Maison Louis. I know it used to be along here somewhere because I remember years ago noticing the Maison Louis sign outside and then reading in an old music paper that Wee Willie Harris got his hair dyed pink - and sometimes green or orange - there. For some reason I wanted to find out exactly where it was. I asked in all the shops, but no luck. And when I went into a dry cleaners there, the couple running the place was too busy helping a girl try on a pink bridesmaid's dress to talk to me. In the end I managed to track down the address at the council archive library, despite the man on the desk being no help at all. It turned out to be the dry cleaners.

City Dry Cleaners is squeezed between two mini-marts: one painted green and the other blue and covered in Irn-Bru signs. I've never drunk Irn-Bru. It wasn't around when I was a kid, not outside Scotland anyway. My favourite was Tizer - 'Tizer the Appetizer'. Better than Lemonade or Cherryade. We'd buy it off a horse and cart that came round the streets selling bottles of pop and if you took the empty bottle back you'd get a penny refund. Once, at a holiday camp fancy dress contest, my mother wrapped me up in lot of red crepe paper and entered me as a bottle of Tizer. I didn't win a prize. At another holiday camp contest she entered me as Cupid, in a white sort of posing pouch and with cardboard wings and bow and arrow. I've never worn fancy dress since, except once in a junior school production of *Toad of Toad Hall*. I was dressed as a duck – one of the jurors in the courtroom scene – and all I had to do was stand up and say 'Present!' when the usher called my name. The costume was very tight and long after the performance had ended, and all the kids had gone home, there were just me and my mother in an empty changing room, with her tugging at the duck's beak trying to get it off my head.

Before he became a full-time rock 'n' roll singer, Willie worked as a pudding mixer at the Peek Frean's biscuit factory in Bermondsey. I had a job like that once – mixing up the ingredients at an ice cream factory on the Isle of Wight.

I've a friend called Frean. He's the Peek Frean founder's great-great-grandson, but has never had anything to do with the company or with biscuits. Some time ago he received an opened packet of them in the post with a letter complaining about their quality. He doesn't know how it ended up at his address.

Supreme Motor Cycles is a couple of doors away from City Dry Cleaners. It's one of the shops I went into to find out if they knew about Maison Louis. Lots of blokes working in there and willing to chat, but no real information. 'Before our time,' one said.

When I was a student I rode a motorcycle. This didn't really go with my image, which required a scooter. My first one was a Francis Barnett 197cc - a 'Franny B' - which cost me £20. On its maiden voyage I ran out of petrol and had to push it two miles home. My girlfriend at the time didn't appreciate that if she rode pillion it couldn't get up hills and so I bought a bigger one – an Ariel Red Hunter 350cc – from an architecture student I shared digs with. But this one was always breaking down and when I moved to London I was glad to get rid of it.

Not long ago I walked out of a Cork Street gallery and crossed the road in front of a motorcycle. I ended up in A&E where they stitched my face up. At the hospital a policeman asked me if I'd contacted anyone at home and I told him that I didn't dare. He told me that if I didn't phone my wife and tell her about the accident then he'd have to put me down in his report as a missing person, which would mean a lot more paperwork for him.

Past the shops there's a park. The land was donated to the London County Council in the 1930s by the newspaper tycoon Lord Rothermere, to be made into the Geraldine Mary Harmsworth Park, in memory of his mother, for the benefit of the 'splendid struggling mothers of Southwark'.

When the Three Stags pub across from the park used to have an art gallery on its second floor, I once met there one of my old students at the private view of a group exhibition he was in. He told me that he was still living with his parents in Billericay. When he graduated from his MA course, Charles Saatchi bought all the paintings in his degree show, but never exhibited any of them. His paintings were all grey monochromes – something to do with British imperialism. Nowadays I don't really enjoy private views. It's difficult to look at the work because the gallery's crowded out with people much younger than me, most of whom I don't know. They used to be fun. I remember one where an abstract painter kicked a figurative sculptor in the balls and another when the same sculptor sent someone dressed like a motorcycle messenger over to tell me that 'Kevin wants to see you outside'. I started waving a bottle at him and nothing much happened.

Four doors past the pub is a Georgian house with a blue door and with a blue plaque on the wall. This is where Captain William Bligh lived when he returned to England after surviving the mutiny on his ship the *Bounty*. It's now the 'Captain Bligh Guest House'.

When I was a student, I saw *Mutiny on the Bounty* at a cinema in Portsmouth, probably because Marlon Brando was in it. I didn't think much of the film, though I liked the look of Princess Maimiti. And so did Brando, because he married the actor who played her – Tarita Teriipaia. Apparently the film is full of historical innacuracies.

One of the ships that William Bligh captained after the *Bounty* was *HMS Warrior*, which was built in Portsmouth dockyard.

The Peek Frean factory closed down in 1989 after 130 years and having introduced Garibaldi and Bourbon biscuits to the world. I never liked those sorts when I used to eat biscuits. It had to be either chocolate digestives or else ginger nuts because they didn't fall to bits when you dipped them in your tea.

I'd drive past the biscuit factory traveling to and from the East London college where I worked. Once someone at the college opened a door too hard into my hand and smashed it. Private health care came with the job and, as the pay was poor, to get my own back I made sure I was treated privately for a series of quite minor ailments, although really that was against my principles. Along from Bligh's house was a private hospital and that's where I had physiotherapy on my hand. The treatment involved the physiotherapist massaging my thumb with an electrical gadget. Neither of us seemed very optimistic that this would work. She was cynical about the hospital and indiscreet about her other patients. She told me that one of her patients, a well-known TV presenter and architecture critic, was paranoid about anything to do with death and insisted on her covering up the plastic skeleton which stood staring at us in the corner of the treatment room. My thumb's still bad. And now, after recently having had cortisone injections, it grinds when I move it up and down.

Willie left Peek Frean's in 1956 and became the resident pianist at the 2i's Coffee Bar in Old Compton Street in Soho. The 2i's was where British rock 'n' roll began. Three Iranian brothers originally owned the coffee bar and so it was called the 3i's. It was renamed when one of the brothers returned home. Then two Australian ex-wrestlers - one of them was Paul Lincoln, who used to call himself Dr. Death - took the place over and started putting on live music in the basement with skiffle groups and then rock 'n' roll singers. Cliff Richard, Johnny Kidd, Adam Faith, Hank Marvin, Terry Dene, Marty Wilde, Vince Eager and Screaming Lord Sutch all played there.

A friend I taught with at an architectural school once played guitar in Sutch's backing band, the Savages. At this school I once sat in on a review of a project where the brief was to design a small museum, to include living quarters for the caretaker. An Iranian student presented a model of a square building with a bungalow stuck on top for the caretaker. During his review he said that if the tutors didn't like the bungalow he'd get rid of it and then, in front of everyone, he smashed his fist down through the model.

When the 2i's closed down it became Le Bistingo restaurant. It's where I ate frog's legs for the first time and, I think, the last. Now it's the Boulevard Bar. A green plaque outside says it's the 'Birthplace of British rock 'n' roll and the popular music industry'.

In the year that Willie started his rock 'n' roll career, the two Russian leaders, Bulganin and Krushchev, visited Britain on warships which docked at Portsmouth and which were open to the public to visit. We kids went along and cadged red star badges and cigarettes off the sailors. But the cigarettes – mostly hollow cardboard tubes – I found unsmokeable. And the Christian Brother teachers at our school forbad us to possess the badges because communists murdered priests.

Every year they have Navy Days in the dockyard. As a fourteen-year-old I went there with two friends. It must have been on a Sunday, because our town was deserted when we sneaked up the alley behind Brickwood's brewery and Barry stood on Ron's shoulders and pinched bottles of brown ale through a barred window while I kept lookout. We then drank them on the train to Portsmouth.

Willie became famous when he appeared on *6-5 Special*. This was the first pop music show on TV. As we didn't have a TV then, I went round my friend's house every Saturday evening to watch it. But it was often disappointing. The two presenters were a bit posh and the regular band was Don Lang and his Frantic Five. Don was a chubby trombone player and the band wasn't very frantic, so not very inspirational. And George Melly was always on, with his bad haircut, awful sweaters and boring songs. There was a lot of skiffle and trad jazz, but not much rock 'n' roll. If you were lucky, Lonnie Donegan or Tommy Steele would appear.

The Imperial War Museum stands in the middle of the park. I once went to the library there to see if I could find out anything about my father's World War II record.

My father is buried in Mook military cemetery in Holland. I visited it on a British Legion trip when I was ten years old and my mother was angry with me because I'd decided to get a crew cut a few days before we left. It was the first time we'd flown in a plane. We stayed with a Dutch family in Nijmegen and the father drove us around in his car. I'd never ridden in a car before and I was fascinated by the cigarette lighter in the dashboard. The daughter tried to teach me to play Monopoly, but as we couldn't speak each other's language it was a waste of time. I went back to the cemetery more recently and it was much smaller than I remembered.

Willie was 5ft 2ins tall, with wild hair that he insured for £12,000. He wore a red drape jacket many sizes too big for him, tight drainpipe trousers, crepe-soled shoes (brothel-creepers) and a huge polka-dot bow tie. Little Richard must have inspired him - they were both short, eccentric piano players with mad haircuts. But Willie was in a lower league really. A bit like Cliff Richard copying Elvis's sneer.

Maison Louis went to a lot of trouble to get Willie's hair colour right. At first it didn't go to plan - it was more of a gingery colour that went unnoticed when Willie went out into the street. It took four or five weeks to get the colour that he wanted which was a vivid pink to match his socks. I once had a pair of fluorescent pink socks and fluorescent green ones as well.

In the 1930s, Rothermere's newspapers called for an alliance with Nazi Germany and strongly supported appeasement. When Hitler came to power, Rothermere wrote in the *Daily Mail*:

> *The German nation was rapidly falling under the control of its alien elements. In the last days of the pre-Hitler regime there were twenty times as many Jewish Government officials in Germany as had existed before the war. Israelites of international attachments were insinuating themselves into key positions in the German administrative machine. Three German Ministers only had direct relations with the Press, but*

> *in each case the official responsible for conveying news and interpreting policy to the public was a Jew.'*

Rothermere also visited and corresponded with Hitler. He expressed the hope that 'Adolf the Great' would become a popular figure in Britain and noted that his work was 'great and superhuman'. He also championed the British Union of Fascists. Rothermere wrote a *Daily Mail* editorial entitled 'Hurrah for the Blackshirts', praising their leader Oswald Mosley for his 'sound, commonsense doctrine'.

In 2002 a Holocaust Memorial Tree was planted in the park.

Tommy Steele was the most famous 2i's rock 'n' roller. Like Willie, he came from Bermondsey. He wore a crew neck sweater with a band of musical notes across the front. I asked my mother to knit me one, but she wouldn't. As a kid I lived on the Isle of Wight and one summer it was big news because Tommy had flown there for a holiday. I was on the beach one day and noticed that Tommy was sitting in the cafe having a drink. Thinking I'd impress him I went up to the cafe jukebox and put on *Little Star* by the Elegants (or perhaps it was *Three Stars* by Eddie Cochran). He didn't seem to notice. By then, his records were a bit wanky – things like *Little White Bull*.

Round the corner from The Three Stags is the college where I once took a poetry course run by a tall American woman with long dyed black hair who wore clothes that never really matched. She said my efforts were a bit too biased towards the visual and always rather impersonal. I had mixed feelings about that. Or I didn't know what to think. I liked concrete poetry, something unfamiliar to her.

The college had a gallery attached to it. I saw a print exhibition there once. Maggi Hambling the painter was sitting at a table tin the corner talking to a man in a very loud voice. She once painted a portrait of George Melly and she was in an art quiz TV programme with him. One of the exhibitors was the wife of the person who injured my hand. She worked in my department and on the days I wasn't in she'd tidy up my desk, which really annoyed me.

Rothermere was a strong opponent of Soviet communism. Again in the *Daily Mail* he wrote:
> *'The sturdy young Nazis of Germany are Europe's guardians against the Communist danger... The diversion of Germany's reserves of energies and organizing ability into Bolshevik Russia would help to restore the Russian people to a civilized existence, and perhaps turn the tide of world trade once more towards prosperity.'*

In 1999 the Soviet War memorial was unveiled in the park.

We never had the *Daily Mail* at home. It was always the *Daily Express*. My grandmother took the *Daily Mirror* because that was the Labour paper. She always voted Labour because of being humiliated by the Conservative government's means test in the 1930s. My mother bought the Catholic newspaper *The Universe* at church every Sunday but, after she read *Red Star Over China* by Edgar Snow, she started subscribing to *Soviet Weekly*. She said she wanted a balanced view of things.

The museum building used to be the Royal Bethlem Hospital, a lunatic asylum better known as Bedlam. In the 18th century people went there to laugh at the patients. The entry charge was one penny, but free on the first Tuesday of the month.

Hercules House is in the next street. It once housed the Central Office of Information. Some time ago I went there to track down a documentary film called *Days of Our Youth*. It featured my wife wearing very thick black false eyelashes. One scene was supposed to be a party. She'd gathered all her friends and we stood around with drinks in some flat one afternoon. It wasn't very exciting. I've never managed to find a copy of this film.

My wife was at art college with Ian Dury. As a student there she lodged for a while in the house of the artist Joe Tilson. Ian Dury married Tilson's daughter, Sophy. One of Dury's songs, *Reasons to be Cheerful,* mentions Wee Willie Harris.

Not long ago I went to a screening of a documentary about Willie. It was held in The Cinema Museum, not far from here. The audience was full of ageing teds and Willie himself was there, signing autographs and chatting to people. The film was terrible.

In 2011 Willie, aged 79, and a blue badge holder, received a £55 fine from Sutton Council for parking for five minutes in a loading bay instead of a disabled bay while he nipped to the toilet. He was having treatment for prostate cancer and got caught short. I walk past City Dry Cleaners on my way to the hospital to have treatment for cancer.

Round the Estate

Four dogs - an Alsatian, a grey mongrel, a brown mongrel and a black-and-white terrier - hurry up the ramp and along the walkway, stopping now and then to sniff at each other or at stains on the wall. They run down the steps at the end of the walkway and across the triangle of grass towards the old play sculptures where they nose around the scraps of litter. The terrier licks at a chip paper and the brown mongrel finds a KFC box with some chicken bones in it which they pull out and chew and crunch. A small boy sitting on one of the sculptures throws a stone at them. The Alsation snarls and jumps up at the scupture, but the boy is too high to reach. When the dog turns round, his companions have disappeared.

A blonde-haired girl gets out of a white Mini, slams the door shut and walks along the path to the high-rise. She looks up at the flats and shouts into her phone. 'Christa!...Are you there Christa?'

A youth sitting on a low wall shouts out to her. 'Is it Christa you're after?'

She ignores him and stands looking at her phone.

'She's not in. She went out half an hour ago.'

The girl returns to the Mini, sits inside with the door open and turns the car radio on loud.

A boy in a black anorak descends the concrete stairway leading down to the underground garages and through the broken-down door at the bottom of the steps. In the third garage along, its door missing, three boys, also in black anoraks, are sitting on stacks of old car tyres. Their bikes lean against the graffiti-covered walls. They look up at the boy.

'Hi Gav – found your dog yet?'

'No, my mum says we'll have to go down Battersea Dog's Home if he don't turn up today.'

The boys fidget and laugh and exchange punches. Two are smoking and all chew gum.

'Where's your bike Gav?'

'Indoors.'

'Get it then, right? Then we'll do something.'

'Okay, if you lot come with me. That mob are still after me for something.'

They stare at him. A cigarette butt is flicked away.

'C'mon then.'

They pick up their bikes, push them past the row of garages and carry them up spiral stairs until they reach the lift doors.

The dogs bump into each other as they trot along together round the back of the flats. One growls and snaps at another's tail. The terrier stops and scratches at a piece of bare earth, turns round two or three times and then squats and shits. A ginger cat appears on a low wall in front of them and the mongrels chase it round a corner, yelping as they go. When the terrier finishes shitting and looks around, the mongrels are nowhere to be seen. He looks in all directions, cocking his head to one side and, after sniffing briefly at his pile of shit, runs off.

They cycle at high speed up and down the landing. Standing up out of their saddles, straining and pushing their legs down as hard as they can. Sometimes they pull their front wheels up off the ground and sometimes they take their feet off the pedals and up onto the handlebars. They collide with each other, scraping their knees against the walls, twisting round, falling off. One boy whoops at the top of his voice, over and over again; another bites his tongue in concentration. They laugh and yell advice. A bike cruches a cardboard box flat, another sends a coke can

37

spinning into the air. A woman's face appears at a window, shouting at them to stop it and clear off and play somewhere else, but they take no notice. Then, from the open doorway of one of the flats, a small smiling child runs out with her hands in the air and a bike immediately knocks her to the ground. The child rolls over shrieking and a man appears at the doorway. He wears a blue flannel dressing gown and is fat and unshaven. Two of the racers have disappeared and the remaining two stand with their eyes fixed on the child lying sobbing beneath a yellow bike. The fat man stares at the child and, without speaking, reaches down, picks up the bike and hurls it over the landing wall. He yanks up the child and pushes it back inside the flat, then strides forward and grabs the nearest racer by the arm.

She twiddles the tuning knob until she finds a different station and then leans back in the seat, humming and picking the remains of the varnish off her left thumbnail and adjusting her hair in the rear-view mirror. There's a loud crash and she jumps up and bangs her head on the car roof. Pushing open the door, she staggers out, rubbing the top of her head and grimacing. A yellow bike has dented the car bonnet and is now sliding off onto the ground.

Gav's head jerks back, then sideways, as the fat man whacks him again and again across one side of his face and then the other, gripping him tightly round the wrist with his other hand.

'I'll fucking murder you if I ever see you on this fucking floor again, you little bastard! D'you hear me?' He shakes him violently. The boy's face is red and lines of blood trickle down from his nostrils. One sleeve of his anorak has ripped apart at the seams. 'You could've killed that kid belting up and down on those fucking bikes! If I catch you at it again it'll be you that goes over the fucking wall, not just the bike!'

The other boy stands some distance away, by the stairs. His face is white as he stares open-mouthed at the beating and he grips his bike handlebars tightly.

'Let him go, you fat turd!' he shouts. 'His brothers'll do you over proper and smash your place up, you big cunt!'

The fat man pulls the boy's hair until his face is close up against his. 'D'you understand me?'

Gav nods his head. Snot and tears mingle with the blood now smearing his face. The fat man shakes him once more and pushes him free, kicking at him with his slippered foot. The crying boy stumbles away towards his friend and they disappear down the stairwell. The fat man leans over the balcony wall, panting heavily.

The youth runs across to where the girl stands staring at the mini. 'I saw what happened. It came from the eighth floor. Somebody must've chucked it over.'

She puts her hands on her hips, glances up and then back down again, slowly shaking her head. 'It's only just had a re-spray.'

'It must've been some kid. Why don't you call the police?'

'What would they do?'

'Well…you should let'm know. If you want to claim insurance you've gotta let'm know.'

'I'd lose me no-claims.'

The youth puts his hands in his pockets and looks up at the eighth floor. 'You could take the bike up there and perhaps see what kid did it. Maybe get his folks to cough up to fix the car.'

'Some hope.'

'You never know. If you threatened to call the police you might get something off them.'

'I dunno.'

'I'll go up there with you if you want.'

She shrugs. 'Okay.'

The old couple sit side by side on the settee. He sips tea and now and then she glances up at the television.

'Christ almighty, what's that racket?' says the man, putting his cup and saucer down on the small table beside him. He picks up the remote control from the settee arm and points it at the television, which goes silent. They both cock their ears towards the window.

'Another row,' says the woman.

'Always bloody rows.' Pushing himself to his feet he walks over to the window and presses his nose against the glass.

'Go out on and have a look.'

He opens the door, walks out onto the balcony and looks over the edge. 'Looks like somebody's chucked a bike over the side and it landed on a car. Somebody should phone the police.'

He walks back into the flat. 'Gaw it's windy out there.'

'Where's the dog gone, by the way?' asks the woman.

Gav runs down the stairwell with his friend carrying his bike and trying to keep up. When they reach the ground floor Gav wipes the blood and snot off his face with his sleeve.

'Look at this rip. That fucker's ruined my fucking jacket.'

He looks around. 'And where's my bike? It should've landed here.'

'I can't see it,' says his friend. 'Somebody must've gone off with it.'

'My dad'll kill me. They only got it for me a couple of weeks ago. For my birthday.'

'P'raps one of the lads picked it up.'

'Maybe...Let's go find them.' He suddenly stops. 'Hang about, that's our dog over there. Hey, Terry! C'mere! Terry! Good boy! Here boy!'

The terrier looks up from a pile of crusts lying on the grass. He stares at the two boys, jumps over a low railing and walks away from them.

'Terry! I said come here! They run towards the dog and it turns to face them and squeezes back through the railing, its tail starting to slowly wag. The boy reaches it and grabs its collar. 'Where've you been you little sod?'

'Fuck me Gav, he looks a right mess.'

'Yeah, bet we both do. But if I take him home p'raps there won't be so much of a row about the bike.'

They walk off, one pushing his bike and the other stooping as he drags along the terrier.

'I'm pretty sure it was this floor,' says the youth as they get out of the lift and look along the landing where a fat man in a blue dressing-gown is leaning against the balcony wall.

'That bloke must've seen what happened…Oi mate!'

The youth walks towards the man, carrying the bike under one arm. The blonde girl stays by the lift door, smoking a cigarette.

'Scuse me mate, but some kid slung this bike over the side and we reckon it came from this floor. Did you see who it was?'

The man looks at the youth, then at the bike and back at the youth.

'She needs to find out who it was. Landed on her car. It was a bloody stupid thing to do.'

The man shouts, grabs the bike and throws it over the side. Then he turns round, walks into his flat and slams the door shut behind him. The youth stares at the door, then at the girl. She sighs, drops her cigarette end to the floor, squashes it with her toe and presses the lift button.

The youth, walks slowly back to join the girl, who says nothing.

'Quiet today.'

The taller of the two looks at his watch. 'Give it another twenty minutes and then we'll wander back to the station.'

'Hang on, what's that shouting all about? Where's it coming from?'

'Can't imagine.'

'Somewhere up there. S'pose we'd better take a look…You go up the back stairs and I'll try the lift.'

They separate, the taller one walking into the building. The shorter one suddenly falls to the ground and lies there motionless beneath a bright yellow bicycle.

The two mongrels come round the corner and stop to look at a policeman lying on the ground with a bicycle on top of him. While the brown one concentrates on pissing against a wall, the grey one spies the ginger cat again and disappears after it.

As they wait for the lift, the blonde girl lights up another cigarette.

'What d'you reckon then? Get the police?'

'I'll get Steve to fix the car. Where's the bloody lift?'

'What did you want Christa for, anyway?'

She frowns at him. 'Do what?'

'Christa...You were looking for her.'

'To ask her if she'd seen our dog. It got out this morning and my dad asked me to see if I could find it.'

The lift doors open and they get in.

The fat man stands against the sink, his hands in his dressing-gown pockets, looking at the little girl sitting on a chair in the kitchen, sniffing as she eats a bag of crisps. Her mother kneels on the floor in front of her, checking each part of her body. She reaches up to the table for a sticking plaster which she smoothes over the large graze on the child's knee. Then another on the elbow.

'Why did you let her get out? I thought you were supposed to be keeping an eye on her. She could've been hurt real bad.'

He pulls a face. 'Why did you let her out, you mean. What were you up to?'

'Cooking your bloody dinner, that's what.'

The little girl starts sobbing and the mother reaches up, holds her head and kisses the top of it.

'You've got nothing else to do. Look - you're not even dressed yet. It wouldn't hurt to keep an eye on her now and then. I knew something would happen with those kids tearing up and down the landing like that. I'm always telling them to clear off but they just give me a load of lip.'

'I don't think they'll back here again.'

'Thumping them's no good. You should call the police.'

'Mummy, I've finished my crisps!'

'And Rebel got out again this morning.'

'He'll be okay…he knows his way back.'

'What's the use of having a dog if he's always running around the estate? He'll get run over or something.' She kisses the little girl's cheek. 'Like Zoë did.'

The fat man puffs out his cheeks and groans. 'I've had enough of this. I'll get some clothes on then I'm off out.'

'What about your dinner?'

As the lift doors open they notice people gathering beside the Mini. When they reach it they see the yellow bike lying in front of the car beside a policeman stretched out on the ground.

'Has somebody called an ambulance?' asks a woman. 'Or the police?'

'The bike must've landed right on his head.'

'Is he dead?'

'Which floor did it come from?'

The girl turns to the youth. 'I'm not getting involved in all this.' She unlocks the car door, climbs in, starts the engine, beeps at the people to move out of the way and then drives off through them towards the main road. Rounding a corner, she notices a brown mongrel dog standing on the pavement, barking. She stops the car and gets out.

'Billy!'

The mongrel goes quiet and turns round. His tail droops and he looks up at the girl with lowered eyes. She opens the passenger door.

'Get in the car you bugger! Where've you been?'

Billy clambers into the car. The girl sits beside him and they drive away.

The fat man leaves the lift and turns left, ignoring the crowd standing over to his right and discussing something on the ground. He heads for the Grosvenor Arms and at the crossroads he stops and folds his arms as an Alsation dog bounds towards him.

'Rebel, you bastard! What you been doing?'

The Alsation stops in the middle of the road, its tongue out and its tail wagging.

'Where you bin, eh? Come here, you silly bugger.'

A black Mini comes round the corner. It swerves to avoid the Alsation and screeches across the road, crunching into a post box.

The grey mongrel stands alone on the triangle of grass outside the tenants' hall, barking non-stop. He looks left and right and all around, but the others are nowhere to be seen. Every time he barks his front paws leave the ground. Passers-by shout at him to shut up but he ignores them and carries on barking.

Footnotes '59

I Go Ape, written by Neil Sedaka and Howard Greenfield and sung by Sedaka, reaches number 9 in the UK Singles Chart in May 1959.

A derailleur gear on a bicycle consists of a chain, sprockets of different sizes and a moveable chain-guide that is operated remotely by a cable attached to a lever. When the rider operates the lever while pedalling, the change in cable tension moves the chain-guide from side to side, 'derailing' the chain onto different sprockets.

Calling someone 'a wanker', meaning one who masturbates, is a popular insult. It can be directed at someone out of earshot by a one-handed gesture performed by curling the fingers of the hand into a loose fist and moving the hand back and forth to mime male masturbation.

The word 'fag', meaning a cigarette, derives from 'fag-end', a sailing term for a rope that was frayed and useless at the end. Cigarettes have a non-smokable butt at one end so the word 'fag' got applied to the butts and ended up being used for the whole cigarette.

Building crystal sets has become popular amongst young boys and hobbyists. The simplest type of radio receiver, it runs on the power received from radio waves by a long wire antenna and needs neither battery nor mains power, whilst tuning is through a coil of copper wire. The set gets its name from its most important component, known as a crystal detector, made with a piece of crystalline mineral such as galena. Crystal sets produce rather weak sound, must be listened to with earphones, and can only pick up stations within a limited range.

Radio Luxembourg began broadcasting to the UK in 1933 and attracted large audiences with its programmes of popular entertainment, circumventing the BBC's monopoly of radio broadcasting, its restrictions on the amount of records that could be played and its ban on advertising. Radio Luxembourg now targets the teenage market and most of the station's output is the playing of pop records. It broadcasts on a medium wave frequency of 208 metres (1439 kHz) and because this signal can be received satisfactorily in the UK only after dark, when it is able to strike the ionosphere and bounce back to the British Isles, its programmes are confined to the evening after 6pm.

After World War II, the AFN (American Forces Network) began to broadcast from American bases in Europe (particularly Germany) to serve American service personnel and their families stationed at bases overseas. As American music is very popular, but rarely played on most of the state operated European stations, it also attracts civilian audiences, Broadcasts are on shortwave bands and reception in the UK is often difficult.

Lambert & Butler's inexpensive Domino cigarettes are sold in open-topped maroon and cream paper packets, shaped and marked like a domino piece and containing four cigarettes. They cost sixpence.

'Minge' is a slang term for vagina.

Reveille is a popular weekly tabloid newspaper launched in 1940 and published by IPC Newspapers Ltd. It regularly features pin-up photographs.

Liquorice allsorts are sweets sold as a mixture and are made of liquorice, sugar, coconut, aniseed jelly, fruit flavourings, and gelatine. The George Bassett Company first produced them in Sheffield in 1899. A Bassett sales representative dropped a tray of samples he was showing a client, mixing up the various sweets. He and the client were intrigued by the new creation and the company began to mass-produce the allsorts which became very popular.

The Leeds firm, J Hepworth & Son, founded in 1864, is a men's clothing and tailoring firm which has grown into a chain of 350 High Street outlets throughout the UK.

Burton is a UK high street clothing retailer founded by Montague Burton in Chesterfield in 1903. After World War II, Burton offered men the chance to buy an outfit comprising jacket, trousers, waistcoat, shirt and underwear, which together became known as 'The Full Monty'. The company is the largest multiple tailor in the world.

A 'bum-freezer', or Italian jacket, is a short, narrow-lapelled, three-button jacket. As a fashion item for young men, it has begun to supersede the fingertip-length 'drape' jacket.

A petty officer is a non-commissioned officer in the navy, equivalent in rank to an army sergeant.

The Norton Dominator is a twin cylinder motorcycle made by the Norton Motorcycle Company of Birmingham. The 500 cc *Model 88* was introduced in 1956 alongside the larger capacity 597cc *Model 99*. Norton motorcycles compete with those built by Triumph in Meriden, West Midlands, particularly the *Thunderbird* and *Tiger* models.

Don and Phil Everly, the Everly Brothers, are an American rock 'n' roll duo. Their hit records in the UK this year include *Problems* and *Poor Jenny*.

In 1953, because UK import restrictions meant that manufactured goods from abroad could only be sold if at least 53% of the content was British made, the Ilford-based Balfour Engineering Company set up an agreement with the Automatic Musical Instrument Company of the USA (AMi) to build jukeboxes in the UK using existing American designs and importing some of the AMi components, whilst manufacturing others in the UK. These machines are called BAL-Ami and one of their most popular models is the 1958 I200M which holds 100 discs in a rotating carousel. It is notable for its pink and charcoal colouring, lots of chrome features and curved-glass front.

Beat the Clock is a game show section of ITV's popular *Sunday Night at the London Palladium* programme, hosted by the compere Bruce Forsyth.

The Coasters, an American doo-wop/rhythm & blues vocal group have had a string of hits, often novelty songs written by Jerry Lieber and Mike Stoller and featuring King Curtis on tenor saxophone. Their biggest UK success is *Charlie Brown*.

Decca Records use the label 'London American Recordings' to release on the UK market American labels which the company license, such as Imperial, Chess, Dot, Atlantic, Speciality and Sun. Featured artists include Fats Domino, Clyde McPhatter, Johnny Cash, The Coasters, Johnny & the Hurricanes, Chuck Berry, Dee Clark, Eddie Cochran, Duane Eddy, Chuck Willis, Bo Diddley, Larry Williams, Jerry Lee Lewis and Roy Orbison.

MGM Records is a record label started by the Metro-Goldwyn-Mayer film studio in 1946, to release soundtrack albums of their musical films. It has become a pop label featuring such artists as Tommy Edwards, Connie Francis, The Impalas, Conway Twitty and Marvin Rainwater.

The Screaming Skull is a 1958 American horror film directed by Alex Nicol and based on a short story by Francis Marion Crawford in which a neurotic woman believes she is being haunted by the ghost of her husband's previous wife. The film opens with a promise by American International Pictures that anyone who dies of fright while watching the film will be given a free burial.

Cage of Doom, also known as The *Girl from 5,000 A.D.* and *Terror from the Year 5000*, is an American science fiction film written and directed by Robert J. Gurney. The film tells of a time machine made by two scientists that unexpectantly brings back a deformed woman from 5200 AD. The woman wants to take healthy males back with her to the future, which has been devastated by radioactivity, but the scientists foil her plans.

Bo Diddley is an American rhythm and blues vocalist, guitarist and songwriter. The hard-edged electric guitar sound in his records, along with his signature beat (a basic, five-accent rhythm) has become a cornerstone of rock 'n' roll and blues. He recorded *Who Do You Love* in 1956.

Oh Boy! is an ITV music show for teenagers. Broadcast live on Saturday evenings from 6-6.30 pm. Each week *Oh Boy!* features resident artists - Cliff Richard, Marty Wilde and Cuddly Dudley - plus guests such as Billy Fury and Lonnie Donegan with occasional US stars such as Conway Twitty and Brenda Lee. The artists are supported by the house band, Lord

Rockingham's XI, and the singing and dancing of The Vernons Girls and the Dallas Boys.

A 'Boston' is a man's haircut in which the hair is cut horizontally at the nape of the neck.

A nickname for a penis is 'John Thomas'. So, 'Johnny', short for 'Rubber Johnny', is a nickname for a condom.

Brown ale is a type of bottled beer with a dark amber or brown colour. Those from northeastern England tend to be strong and malty, often nutty, while those from southern England are usually darker, sweeter and lower in alcohol.

In the FA Cup Final at Wembley, Nottingham Forest beats Luton Town 2-1 with goals from Roy Dwight and Tommy Wilson, Dave Pacey scoring Luton's goal. There are a large number of injury stoppages in the game and Roy Dwight is carried off the pitch after 33 minutes with a broken leg. The game is televised live on the BBC *Grandstand* programme, which introduces score captions into a cup final broadcast for the first time. During the game the Forest fans are heard to sing the theme tune to the television programme *Robin Hood*, the first time that popular television culture has made its way into a terrace song during a cup final.

Apprenticeship is a system whereby young people learn a craft or trade while working for and being trained by, an employer, providing a supply of young people seeking to enter vocational careers by offering transferable skills and knowledge. With a buoyant labour market and readily available jobs and apprenticeships, approximately one third of boys leaving school become apprentices. The attraction, despite very low pay and the presence of higher-paid starting jobs for school leavers, is the traditional one of getting a trade that will lead eventually to better prospects. They are usually for a period of five years. Apprentices also attend a local technical college while still being paid by the employer, usually for one day and one evening a week studying for City and Guilds or the Ordinary National Certificate.

The General Certificate of Education (GCE) is an academic qualification for schoolchildren introduced in 1951 to cater for the increased range of subjects available to pupils after the raising of the school leaving age from 14 to 15 in 1947. It comprises two levels: the Ordinary Level (O Level), normally taken at age 15 and the Advanced Level (A Level) taken two years later by sixth-form students.

The 1944 Education Act created a system in which children are tested and streamed at the age of eleven. The eleven-plus examination, taken in the final year of primary schooling, determines which children go to which schools. Those deemed intellectually able, suited for an academic curriculum, are sent to grammar schools. The three-quarters majority are educated in secondary modern schools where education focuses on basic subjects such as arithmetic and practical skills such as woodworking for boys and cookery for girls. Secondary moderns are inadequately funded and generally deprived of both resources and good teachers and are seen as the school for failures, there to learn rudimentary skills before going on to factory or menial jobs.

MGM's *Jailhouse Rock*, made in 1957 and directed by Richard Thorpe, was Elvis Presley's third film. Jerry Leiber and Mike Stoller created the soundtrack and their songs included *Treat Me Nice*, *Baby I Don't Care* and *Jailhouse Rock*.

The Roman Catholic Church teaches that during Mass, in the ritual, or sacrament, of Holy Communion, the priest changes bread and wine into the body and blood of Christ. A Catholic who wished to receive Communion has to abstain from food and drink from midnight on.

Tiger, a British comic magazine published by IPC Magazines, first appeared in 1954. It features mostly sporting strips, its most popular one being 'Roy of the Rovers' which follows the life of the fictional footballer Roy Race and the team he plays for, Melchester Rovers.

Shortly after the beginning of the celebration of the Roman Catholic Mass, the priest sings, or says, the ancient Greek prayer Kýrie eléison ('Lord have mercy') three times, followed by a threefold Christe eléison (Christ have mercy) and by another threefold Kýrie eléison, each time repeated by the congregation.

Two-Way Family Favourites is broadcast at 12 noon on Sundays on the BBC Light Programme. It is a request programme linking families at home in the UK with British Forces serving in West Germany or elsewhere overseas. Its popularity is due to it being one of the few BBC radio programmes that play records of popular music. Presented by Cliff Michelmore, Jean Metcalfe and, in Cologne, Bill Crozier, its signature tune is *With A Song in My Heart*. The programme is followed at 1.15 pm by *The Billy Cotton Band Show*. The bandleader, Billy Cotton, starts each show with the cry 'Wakey-Wake-aaaay!' followed by the band's signature tune *Somebody Stole My Gal*.

Russ Conway is a British popular pianist who has had two number one UK chart hits in 1959: *Side Saddle* and *Roulette*. He is a fixture on light entertainment TV and radio shows, appearing regularly on *Sunday Night at the London Palladium* and *The Billy Cotton Band Show*.

The *News of the World* is a Sunday newspaper published in the UK. Founded in 1843, it is the biggest-selling newspaper in the world with a weekly sale of over 8 million copies.

Chuck Berry is an American guitarist, singer and songwriter and one of the pioneers of rock 'n' roll. With songs such as *Maybellene*, *Roll Over Beethoven* and *Johnny B. Goode* he has developed rhythm and blues into the major elements that make rock 'n' roll distinctive, with lyrics focusing on teen life and consumerism and utilizing guitar solos and showmanship.

A 'chippie' is a carpenter.

Weights are an inexpensive brand of cigarette manufactured by the John Player Company owned by Imperial Tobacco.

A 'sparks' is an electrician.

People smoke over 106 million cigarettes in the UK every year and Player's Medium Navy Cut is one of the most popular brands. They are produced in the Nottingham factory of John Player & Sons, part of the Imperial Tobacco Company.

Ten bob is ten shillings (half of £1). The usage of bob for shilling dates back to the late 1700s but its origin is not known for sure.

The *Daily Herald* is a left-wing British daily newspaper that at one time was the world's best-selling paper, with sales of 2 million. Its sales have declined as its largely working class readership is not considered a valuable advertising market.

Polos were first manufactured by Rowntree's in 1948 and quickly became the UK's best selling mint flavoured sweet. The name comes from the word 'polar' to suggest the cool and fresh feeling one gets from sucking the sweet. A Polo is 1.9 cm in diameter, 0.4 cm deep and has a 0.8 cm wide hole in the middle, hence its advertising slogan *The Mint with the Hole*. The Polo is white in colour with the word 'POLO' embossed twice on one side around the ring and sold in individual packs of 23 mints, the tube being tightly wrapped with aluminium foil backed paper underneath a green and blue paper wrapper.

Art Outings

One

I place my money in the tray. The driver looks at it and says he has no change and I tell him that is all I have. He mutters something and I pick up the money, go and sit down and start to read the paper. After a few moments I notice that we aren't moving, that the driver is looking over his shoulder at me and the other passengers are staring at me. I ask the driver if he wants me to get off and he says: 'No, just get some change.' I walk down the bus, asking people for change and a man gives me some. Then I pay the driver and get my ticket.

At the next stop a gang of youths board. They all run upstairs, most of them without paying the fare. Then a very loud noise starts from above which someone next to me says is due to the stamping of feet. One woman suggests calling 999, a family discusses whether to get a taxi, the driver says he's looking for a police car and I get off the bus.

It's a pleasant day for a walk by the river. There's a few alcoholics and works of art about. I pass an ancient building I've never noticed before, encircled by a moat with large black fish swimming around in it. An old man in a black beret is throwing bread to them.

Statues of historically important men ring the square. A 1940s-looking youth with spiky greased hair and strange eyes is sitting on a bench and says something to me as I pass. I know he's asking me from money, but I pretend to think he wants to know the time. I glance at my watch and tell him it's just gone twelve o'clock.

Two

Making sure I have everything, including my umbrella (the weather report has mentioned rain), I leave the house.

Two buses come along together. I board the second one and go upstairs where an old man sitting behind me has an attack of hiccups. I get off at the Elephant and Castle to change buses and have difficulty finding the right stop.

This bus is much more crowded. Two small girls are very noisy and two small boys in front of them keep climbing over the seats and calling everything 'fucking' this and 'fucking' that. Then they start laughing at someone with a big nose. The scenery is unpleasant. I read once that only in Britain do people complain about having to live in high-rise flats.

When I get there, I look in one or two shop windows to kill some time and then walk down an almost aesthetically pleasing road. I remind myself of what I have to buy before I go home: an Easter egg and some mushrooms.

At first I think the abrupt librarian isn't on duty. But then I see him. I'm determined to be more organized this time and to stick at it.

I'm sitting opposite an eccentric old woman. She asks the librarian to fetch her two very large dictionaries and then goes over each page with her forefinger, talking very loudly to herself and staring around at everyone, particularly at the African sitting beside me with his biblical books.

A coincidence. My book falls open at exactly the page I want: 'Crime'.

I manage to get a lot done and am quite pleased with myself. As I leave, I pass the abrupt librarian and look away to avoid embarrassment.

I pick up an *Evening Standard* and then go into an art shop and buy three 2H pencils (my current favourite).

Three

I'm becoming aware that I might appear suspicious. Passers-by must think I'm photographing some odd buildings – nothing of any architectural or historical interest. I look quite guilty when a policeman strolls by and for a moment I think he might say something.

Preparing answers should anyone ask what I'm up to, I arrive at six possibilities:

1. What's the problem?

2. It's a free country.

3. I didn't know this was against the law.

4. I'm studying architecture.

5. I'm an artist.

6. Comment? (French).

It's my first time out in my new trousers. A lorry driver shouts something at me. I don't catch what he says, but it makes me jump.

To begin with I'm very particular. No cars or people blocking the view, each shot straight on, the same reading each time. But that becomes so difficult that I give up bothering so much. For a start there's the problem of my reflection in the windows; then the sun comes out and messes up the readings. Then the traffic and the tourists increase during the morning.

I feel hungry twice. The second time, thinking I can grab a coffee and a Bounty Bar, I look in at some cafes. But as it's now lunchtime, they're all too crowded, so I don't bother.

At around 1.30 I run out of enthusiasm and, to a lesser extent, galleries.

Four

Leaning on his gate, the man who lives opposite asks me if I'm off to get some exercise. I laugh, reply yes and cycle off. A few minutes later I make a bad right turn and the driver of a hooting car behind me screams: 'Why don't you fucking signal?' as he passes me on the left.

The first one is nearby. But I don't bother with it because it's behind a locked gate and an Alsatian is lying there beside two men stripped to their waists and washing a car. I guess they're the caretakers. Or one of them is.

My next stop is a small park. I sit down on the grass just inside the entrance to get my bearings and jot a few things down in my notebook. Then I'm off again.

Reaching the estate, I ride round and through it twice because I can't find what I'm looking for in such a big place. When I do find it, one or two kids look at me.

The day is very hot. The shirt I'm wearing is too thick and I'm thirsty.

The second estate isn't where I thought it would be. I ride around for a while, searching in vain. In a road wet from the morning's market and full of men clearing up the rubbish, I ask two boys for directions. The one in the red shirt laughs artfully at his friend and tells me I'm miles out of my way. In fact it isn't very far and I discover it by pure chance.

Outside the estate I buy a vanilla ice cream from an Italian in a van and tread on the toe of the woman behind me in the queue, but she's all right about it. I sit on a wall to eat the ice cream and look up at the top of a grassy hill. Everything is rather pleasant, especially as it's becoming cooler.

Five

Unsure whether or not cycling is allowed, I decide to push it.

Remembering coming here as a child with my Uncle Willie, I sit down on a bench and look at the lake where three youths are trying to capsize a rowing boat they've hired. There aren't too many people about, only a little girl feeding ducks at the water's edge and a few mothers with pushchairs. Despite the weather, I feel vaguely depressed.

I walk on and am surprised to find the first one so soon. It's in very good condition – just a few bird droppings only visible on close inspection.

An old lady begins to throw pieces of bread into the lake and suddenly finds herself with a duck audience. Boys are fishing and running past with their rods. A pity about the traffic noise.

Two kids come along. They stop for a moment when the one with glasses says: 'What's that?' I can't catch the rest of their conversation. A girl walks by with 'Barbara' printed on the front, which I think is quite a coincidence. Then two men with large families stop to chat with each other.

As I stroll on, two boys cycle past. Perhaps cycling isn't prohibited after all. I ask an attendant who's sweeping up leaves if it's allowed.

'No,' he replies.

'Oh, just kids?'

'No, they ain't supposed to either.'

The other one is on the far side of the lake. As I'm about to start, a family arrives and takes their jackets off, as though settling down for the afternoon, and I think I might have to return later. But no – the mother, son and daughter stand together in the middle of it while the father photographs them. Then they gather up their jackets and hurry away.

It's in quite a state. Messages all over it. A crowd of boys appears and one asks me: 'What's it meant to be?' I reply that I don't know. Another boy tells me that people stand in the middle and make a wish. They all leave and another family turns up for another photo session and the mother says: 'Ooh – art.' Then they leave as I leave.

Six

I think I can kill two birds with one stone by popping to the bank and dealing with the art on the way home. Waiting to cross the road, I manage to avoid saying hello to someone I don't want to talk to.

As I unchain my bike from the railings outside the bank, I look at the Securicor guards loading money into their van and wonder if they've ever been robbed.

I go via the street where I was conceived. When I reach the estate a sign says: 'No Cycling', so I get off my bike and push it, noticing other people cycling instead.

It's in quite good condition. Someone has written 'Stephen' in white chalk on the thing itself, a big 'RA' has been painted on the base and an empty fizzy drink can lies at the bottom. When I lean my bike up against a wall, a canary in a cage outside one of the ground floor flats starts chirping very loudly.

Some people watch me: a youth mending his car, a young mother and her child, a kid on a bike, two men passing by. I soon leave.

I've almost reached home when my next-door neighbour runs across the road in front of me. 'Don't run me over with that!' she shouts, laughing.

Seven

After Sunday dinner I spend some time wondering if it's going to rain. And then I think: Why not?

I put on my green coat, sling the camera over my shoulder and wheel the bike through from the kitchen, scaring the cat and making her run upstairs. Then I'm away, with some West Indians staring at me from a car they're mending across the road.

The journey takes about ten minutes. I stop just once – to

look in a shop window I've always meant to look in.

I arrive twenty minutes too early and wonder whether I'll meet someone I know (after all, the art world *is* a small one), but the few people that are there seem to be foreign tourists. Perhaps, like me, people have been concerned about how the weather would turn out.

Cycling back, I stop to look at a sign in a driving school window that says that if you fail your driving test with them they'll give you free lessons until you *do* pass. I can see a driving-wheel machine on a small table in their waiting room.

When I get home I go upstairs to lie down for five minutes. While on the bed I read three or four pages of an autobiography, laugh out loud and get up.

Eight

Because of my operation, I go by tube. I've allowed myself 45 minutes or so to get there, but the eventual journey takes much longer. I have to change trains twice. The second change means leaving the station, crossing a road and entering another station where three trains are waiting to leave. I choose a train and sit down inside. It's the one that leaves third.

At the printers the photos aren't ready, although they were supposed to have been done the day before. 'Try about one o'clock,' says the man.

The day is very hot. There are lots of large American girls in blue jeans and carrying bright orange rucksacks as big as themselves. I go to a library, look at some art magazines and go back to the printers at 1.30. 'Still not ready,' he says, apologising this time. 'Call back at four.' I say I'll come back tomorrow.

Wishing to take an easier route home, I walk back to a different tube station and pass a man lounging in his front room with his feet out the window. He's playing soul music very loudly.

I go into a shop to buy a belt, but all the assistants are standing out on the pavement, staring up the road. Something is happening on the green, but I can't see what. The belts aren't worth buying.

The tube is held up for a long time in the tunnel between Bond Street and Oxford Circus. Perhaps it's a bomb scare. Sitting opposite me is a thin, nervous woman trying to read an art book.

Walking past the town hall, I look at the election results pasted up outside and feel angry.

As I walk home from the station, a large black hearse zooms past. Following right behind it is a Rentokil van.

Nine

I put on my leather jacket, walk out the door and am surprised to find the side rear window of the car smashed in. I stare at it and then realize that there are other people in the street staring at their cars. Their windows have been smashed too. 'It's a fucking kids man,' says a West Indian in a woollen hat. I say I'll phone the police.

This has upset my plans for the afternoon. I go back into the house and phone the police station. 'Oh yes, we've had a lot of reports of damage to cars in that area. We'll send somebody round.'

I take off my jacket, sit down, have a drink and wait.

Two policemen arrive and say that some kid has taken a walk from Clapham to Brixton, smashing the windows of over forty cars on the way.

I finally manage to drive off. Although draughty round the back of my neck from the broken window, the journey isn't too bad because most of the traffic is going the other way. But the engine makes a terrible clanking noise every time I rev it. I can't imagine why.

When I arrive I park under a streetlight and open the bonnet to try to find the cause of the clanking. The air filter has worked loose. Quite an art owning this car.

I've never seen the library so crowded. Mostly old people, but one or two younger men studying hard. I can't find what I'm looking for, or anything of any value, so after an hour I leave.

Ten

Not too much traffic about. This time I don't get lost trying to find the bridge.

As I look for a spare meter, the car stops dead at a narrow junction. Obviously the garage didn't fix the problem. I try turning the key a couple of times, but nothing. And now a car is waiting to get past. Is art worth all this trouble, I wonder. I get out, as does the driver of the car behind, and together we push the car backwards into a spare parking space which luckily is right there. I thank him and he drives off.

The place is just round the corner. Outside, loading a lorry, is the same man who last time told me I had the wrong place.

'Hallo,' he says.

'You were wrong,' I say. 'I had the right place. They do sell them – upstairs.'

'Oh,' he says.

Upstairs a lot of people are standing around not doing too much. I ask whether I can pay for it by card, but the man who seems to be in charge says: 'No, only cash.' I say I don't have enough money on me.

I return to the car, try the key and the engine starts first time. I put some money in the meter and walk to the library.

There are three or four people there – more than usual. I speak to the librarian and she fetches me what I want.

After a couple of hours I become very hungry and also

realize that I should go and feed the meter. An old man sitting nearby has told me that the traffic wardens are pretty hot round here.

Outside it's now dark and raining. As most of the cars have disappeared because people have finished work, I drive to a space where the meter has a spare hour on it and then go back inside.

I stay for another hour, during which time I discover that certain artists had once been very left wing.

Can Man

When my eyes open I blink six times. The ceiling is cream, the same cream. I turn to the clock. That's not working. There are noises somewhere…downstairs. Plates clinking. After a time my feet move sideways down onto the floor and lift me up. Underpants and black jeans are on the chair and I pull them on and then walk along the landing to the bathroom where the mirror shows me a face.

'You ugly stupid bastard,' he tells me.

'Yes,' I reply and turn on the tap. Anti-clockwise. When the water becomes warm I splash some on my face.

'You're no good.' A whisper this time.

'No.'

'You can't even wash yourself properly.'

'I can.'

In the kitchen my mother smiles and nods when I enter and asks me what I want. I think she asks me this every day.

'There's tea in the pot,' she says and I pour some into a mug on the draining board.

'That mug needed washing,' she says. But I don't reply as I sit down at the table. Packets of pills are lined up and she presses out some tablets onto the table.

'You should eat first.' She pushes a plate holding two slices of toast towards me as I shake my head and swallow the pills one by one, washing them down with sips of tea.

'Don't eat that shit,' says the radio.

'I won't.'

'Try and eat something,' she says. 'You don't look well today.'

'She's poisoning you.'

'I know. I can smell it on the toast.'

There's a knife lying on the table. She uses it to cut the bread. It has a red handle. I stroke its blade until she stares at me, slides the knife from under my fingers, picks it up and puts it away in a drawer.

'Are you going to shave today?'

I unlock the door to my room and sit down on the edge of the bed.

My guitar is standing in the corner. 'I'm getting very dusty.'

'I don't want her in here. Looking for things. Stealing.'

'You can't make music anyway. Just stupid noises.'

Once she's gone to work, I put on my boots and my jacket and leave the house. My shoulders squeeze up from the cold. As I walk my arms don't move and stay tight by my sides. I don't look at anyone and I keep the same expression on my face all the time so that no one knows what I'm thinking. The way to the shop is easy: turn left, then right and left at the main road.

The Portuguese men that hate me are leaning against the betting shop window, talking about me in their language. But I pretend not to notice.

There's a queue in the shop. The African behind the counter is plotting on his phone and I stand in the corner to count out my money, away from where the camera can see me.

When there is no queue, the African, still plotting, grins at me. 'The usual?'

He takes four cans off a shelf, puts them into a white plastic bag and hands them to me over the counter. I put the money on the counter, knowing it's clever of me that I can say nothing. Not to him. There's no change.

'He's cheating you, you moron.'

'I know.'

The Portuguese are still there, laughing. Round the corner three schoolgirls walk towards me. They move aside to walk in the road as I pass.
'They're turning around and pointing at you. Because you're ugly and weird.'
The cans clink together, telling me they want to get back to my room, where it's safe.

Stockwell Road Shots

In 1966 the Italian director Michaelangelo Antonioni made the film *Blow-Up*, about a photographer's accidental involvement with a gun murder. In one scene David Hemmings is driving his open-top Rolls Royce along a street in which all the buildings are painted red. This is the Stockwell Road, and the buildings were the premises of the motorcycle dealers Pride & Clarke.

The Brixton Academy used to be The Astoria cinema. I once saw an Andy Warhol film there – *Lonesome Cowboys*. I remember thinking how funny it was and wondering how much of the film was Warhol's and how much Paul Morrissey's. But I don't remember much else about it – the plot or any of the scenes – except someone shooting, or threatening to shoot, Taylor Mead.

Violette Bushell was a pupil at the school in Stockwell Road and as a teenager went dancing at The Swan pub. In 1940 she married Etienne Szabo, a captain in the Free French Army. After he was killed at the Battle of El Alamein in 1942, she joined the Special Operations Executive (SOE) and became a secret agent in occupied France. In 1944 she was captured and tortured by the Gestapo and sent to Ravensbruck concentration camp where she was shot in January 1945.

I get my hair cut at a barber's a few doors away from the Academy. The barber is a Greek Cypriot with a strange haircut – a darkish crop except for a big white fringe in the front. When he's cutting my hair I can feel his stomach pressing into my shoulders. You don't hear too much about Cyprus these days, but when I was a child the news was always full of stories about EOKA shooting British soldiers.

The J-Bar was a nightclub in Stockwell Road. A detached, squarish building painted blue and yellow, it was closed down in October 2006 after a police raid in which drugs and two loaded handguns were found hidden in loudspeakers. That was the latest in a series of incidents at the J-Bar, which included reports of gunshots and on another occasion a large mob throwing bottles and stones at a person who was trying to leave the club.

There's a small hole in the window of the William Hill betting shop. I guess it must be a bullet hole from a couple of days ago, when those kids shot the little girl at the shop next door.

ABM (All Bout Money) is a gang located on and around the Stockwell Park Estate. ABM and the Lambeth-based 031 (O Trey One) gang fell out over a minor issue in 2006-07 and have been in conflict ever since. On 29 March 2011, three 031 members riding bicycles chased two ABM members into the Stockwell Food and Wine Shop on Stockwell Road and fired shots into the shop. They missed the two youths, but bystanders Thusha Kamaleswaran, aged five, was hit in the chest and Roshan Selvakumar, 35, suffered a head wound.

On March 21 2005, at the Brixton Academy in Stockwell Road, gunfire halted a concert by the American rapper Nas. 20 minutes into his show a gun went off at the back of the stalls, then there was a second round of shots which caused pandemonium in the auditorium and a rush for the doors, causing a bottleneck. 30 police, many of them armed, arrived within half an hour, by which time most concertgoers had been evacuated. There were questions as to how a gun could have been smuggled past the security cordon of a bag search and a handheld metal detector.

I usually buy my newspaper in the Stockwell Convenience Store. Whenever I've gone in there the African guy behind the counter is having a mobile phone conversation - I don't think I've ever heard him speak directly to a customer. I glance through the paper as I walk up the road: 'Two Britons shot dead during Florida holiday', 'Rebel fighters have been found shot in the head', 'Syrian forces shoot dead eight protestors'.

A youth wearing a black t-shirt with 'Son of a Gun' printed across it pushes a woman in a wheelchair along the pavement, forcing me to step into the road. The woman's also dressed in black and inhaling rapid, exaggerated puffs of her cigarette. She starts thumping her chest and shouts, 'I'm expecting a shitload!' 'You're paranoid,' says the boy.

In the 18th century, tea was highly taxed and the smuggling of tea into the country was big business. Much of it came from Holland and was distributed from the south coast of England along a network of secret routes to the main market in London, the centre of the official tea trade. The dealers often met with the smugglers at The Swan in the Stockwell Road, near the warehouses, owned or leased by the smuggling gangs, where the tea was stored. The smugglers' route to Stockwell ran across Clapham Common and, one night in 1743, Custom and Excise officers were tipped off about a gang that would be crossing the common with horses loaded with tea. The armed revenue men lay in wait to ambush the gang. The smugglers - said to number more than twenty - arrived and stood their ground when confronted. Outnumbered, the officers retreated as the smugglers fired their guns and moved on with their contraband, cheering as they went.

I pass by the Spiritualist Church. My Aunt Elsie was a spiritualist medium. Her sister, my grandmother, said that she became a spiritualist after my father was killed in the Second

World War, shot at the Battle of the Reichswald in February 1945.

On December 27 1994, Wayne Hutchinson, recently released from a psychiatric hospital, went to Mixes club in Stockwell Road and shot the doorman twice at point-blank range, killing him. The previous day he had blasted the windows of a house on the Stockwell Park Estate with the same sawn-off shotgun. On December 31 he stabbed a man, who happened to be walking along the Stockwell Road, in the chest. The next day he stabbed a man and a woman in a shop in Landor Road, killing the woman. He later told police that he had a gift of knowing when people were 'taking the piss' and that all those people he had attacked over the Christmas period 'deserved what happened'.

I go into a Portuguese café to buy a loaf of bread. There are a lot of Portuguese cafés along this bit of the road and there are always customers in them, drinking coffee and watching football on TV. It wasn't that long ago that Portugal had a full-scale revolution and hardly anyone was killed, just four demonstrators shot by the secret police.

On 22 July 2005 Jean Charles de Menezes, a Brazilian electrician, took the no.2 bus from Brixton, up Stockwell Road and got off outside The Swan. He crossed over Clapham Road, entered the Tube station, walked down the escalator and boarded a train. Three specialist firearms police officers followed him into the carriage and shot him seven times in the head. He died at the scene.

I look in the window of Brixton Cycles, opposite the school. I don't want to buy anything, I just like looking at the bikes and the skateboards. I notice that one of the BMX bikes is called a Bombshell and another a Roadkill.

On 3 May 1922 a war memorial was unveiled on the triangle of common land at the top of Stockwell Road to commemorate the deaths of 574 local men in the First World War. Five of them once lived in Stockwell Road. The architect Frank Twydals Dear designed the memorial, a clock tower built of Portland stone.

The Swan specializes in tribute bands. I often note their names on the posters outside, like *Wham!Duran* and *Guns N Maiden*. When *Frankie Goes to Hollywood* were popular in the 1980s, a band called *Paddy Goes to Holyhead* played there, which I remember made me laugh.

Corners

The two roads cross. The name of one means 'lake of the Welsh' and the other may derive from an old Norman word meaning 'the biter'.

Before the council made the white halt lines more visible, car collisions often happened here. You'd hear a crash, look out the window and see a couple of blokes – usually blokes - getting out of their cars, one looking puzzled and the other angry.

Once there was a little dairy-come-grocery shop here, but it was demolished with all the other houses along that side. Nothing replaced them for years and graffiti-covered rusty corrugated sheeting ran the whole length of the street – until they built a block of sheltered flats for elderly West Indians.

There used to be a shop on every corner: the dairy, three grocery stores, a newsagent and a shoe repairer. Now all that's left is a pub and the laundromat next door to it.

On the next corner, two Portuguese guys are sitting on the wall outside the closed-down Ethiopian restaurant. Ethiopian immigration to Britain started in 1974, when Haile Selassie's government was overthrown by the military and many people were forced from their homes. It increased in 1991 when civil war and continuous political unrest meant a large number of Ethiopians claimed asylum in Britain.

The Portuguese are acting nervous. The tall one is wearing a black jacket and a beanie. The short one, in a shabby grey anorak, keeps shifting to the edge of the pavement and looking up the road. A black guy with braided hair approaches. He's the local dealer, who lives round the corner. He always walks quickly, leaning forward a little - a man with a mission. Shorty crosses the road to meet him and something is palmed as they pass. The dealer strides on and the Portuguese disappear.

Portuguese started to arrive in this area in the 1960s and 1970s during the rule of the dictator Salazar, when the lack of jobs and the threat of military service in African colonial wars meant there was no alternative to looking for work abroad.

Mr. Brown, a Jamaican builder, owned the restaurant building. The restaurant - or perhaps a club – was on the ground floor, though most of the action seemed to be in the basement. A video for some boy band whose name I can't remember was filmed there once.

Scenes from another pop video were shot in the The Marquis of Lorne pub on the corner opposite. This was of Mike Skinner doing a remix of *Banquet* by Bloc Party. I wonder if the pub landlord or the regulars know about the Marquis. In 1871, when the houses round here were being built. he married Queen Victoria's fourth daughter, Princess Louise. The pair tended to live apart, never had children and he was closely associated with men who were known to be gay. The Marquis of Lorne was also the name of a revolver called a 'Suicide Special', one of the many small, cheap revolvers that were made in the USA in the late 1870s.

Mr. Brown also used to own the building on the corner opposite when it was a grocery store run by his wife, who seemed quite a bit younger than him. It had very erratic opening hours – rarely mornings. He built a kind of conservatory or shed on the front of the shop and for a short while this operated as a barber's. But its hours were even more erratic and so customers were infrequent. He sold up, they went back to Jamaica and now the building's been converted into flats.

The West Indian community in Brixton originated in 1948, when a group of over 400 Jamaican immigrants arrived by ship at Tilbury. They were temporarily housed in an air raid shelter in Clapham, not far from the Brixton Employment Exchange, where some of them found work.

On the fourth corner is the special needs school. At playtime the kids' footballs are always flying over the school fence and bouncing into the road. Sometimes, if one lands near me when I happen to be passing, I kick it back.

Governments haven't been able to decide about the kids in these schools. Sometimes they're saying they should be in mainstream schools, because they shouldn't be discriminated against – thought of as being different from other kids. Then they're saying the kids will progress better with special teaching.

Next to the school, reaching to the corner at the end of the street, is a newish block of yellow brick flats where previously stood a decaying grey building functioning as artists' studios. It seemed that you had to be an abstract artist to work there. I looked in at a group show there once and all the sculptures were indistinguishable: big chunks of rust-covered steel welded together. 'Rustism', I thought it should be called. I wasn't sure whether the patina was intentional or because there were so many leaks in the roof. The people working there weren't that friendly – perhaps I didn't look like an abstractionist. When the building became too dilapidated the artists moved out and the druggies took over. The only way they could get in and out was by squeezing through the narrow, high-up windows.

People leave rubbish on one corner. Old mattresses, carpets, floorboards, settees, piles of bricks, dead cats. Anything. They used to leave it on a different corner but, when the council put up a 'Dumping Prohibited' sign there, the rubbish was left on this corner instead.

South Street

No.1

Because it's rusting away so much, it's difficult to read 'South Street' on the sign on the corner of this house It's also covered in dents from some kid shooting at it with an air rifle.

An African couple with their three children used to live here. Once, when they'd left the downstairs front window open, someone climbed through and burgled the place. The father then criss-crossed the window with wire and put up a notice saying: THIS WIRE IS LIVE - DO NOT TOUCH. It wasn't up long before the police told him to take it down.

A Brazilian woman and her two daughters are the tenants now. For a long time the girls' father wasn't allowed to enter the house and on his occasional visits he could only talk to the girls standing at the front door. But now the mother has a new man (who looks exactly like the father) and the two of them walk down the street with his arm over her shoulder.

No.7

The man here is a preacher at a Pentecostal church and on Sunday mornings he leaves holding a big black bible. One of his sons became a well-known rapper and when I chatted to him the other day on one of his visits home he gave me his website address so I could check out his music. But I never did like rap.

No.9

Next door, a couple with a young baby moved into the first floor flat. They became friendly with the woman living directly across the street who also had a young baby. One day this woman, looking out her front bedroom window, noticed the man at his window and waved at him. He then unzipped his trousers and took out his penis.

When that couple moved out, a Haitian man, always dressed in a blue anorak and baseball cap, bought the house, which became very rundown. As well as living there himself, he let out some of the rooms, including the cellar. You could often see or hear arguments between him and his lodgers about rent payments, especially with a very short Portuguese woman who lived there with her family. Sometimes these took place in the street. In the end the council used health and safety regulations to stop him renting and he sold up.

No.13

I once opened the door to a man who showed me a badge, said he was a plain-clothes policeman and asked if he could come in and keep a watch on No.13 from my front window. I looked at the badge and it seemed okay, so I agreed. The people living in this house at the time never appeared very often and I knew nothing about them. He spent about an hour staring out the window and wouldn't tell me what the occupants were suspected of. Probably drugs.

No.17

Every Saturday morning a number of smartly dressed people

meet here. I wondered about this for some time until the man who lives next door at No.15 told me that they're Jehovah's Witnesses.

No.25

Farther up the street lived a couple with their two children, a boy and a girl. The boy never seemed to go to school and the little girl, too young for school, often played in the street on her own. One evening the father came back from the pub to find that the woman had thrown all his clothes out of the upstairs window. He picked up a dustbin and used it to smash all the windows at the front of the house, top and bottom.

No.27

An Italian woman is in the next house along. She's short and stout and walks very slowly. Like a few of the women round here, she once worked in the chemical toilet fluid factory at the end of the street. You could always smell the fumes. Recently her chain-smoking husband, of similar stature and also a slow walker, dropped dead at the wheel of his car parked outside their house. I never got round to telling her I was sorry to hear about him. Their son is back living with her and, having inherited the car, spends a lot of time cleaning it.

No.29

This place always looked in a mess. There were 'Beware of the Dog' signs stuck up in the window, even though the family that lived there never owned a dog. There were six of them. The father was very tall and the mother very short and they had four sons, one fat and three thin. Weeks before each Christmas, one of the thin ones would wear a Santa hat if ever he went out. The fat balding one used to have big rows in the street with his big blonde-haired girlfriend until a stylish, good-looking black girl with a pronounced limp and disabled arm replaced her. Another brother's girlfriend always walked along beside him with her head turned to one side. After a spell of being pushed around in a wheelchair, the father died and then the rest of the family moved out, whereupon the house became the subject of a TV makeover programme.

No.37

A few doors along lived a family with a red-haired boy, about ten years old, who never seemed to go to school but just rode up and down the street on his bike. One day he hanged himself from the banister. Afterwards his older brother came round door-to-door collecting contributions towards his funeral.

No.39

A woman who lives here is always dressed completely in pink. Not just her clothes, but also her shoes, jewellery, hair, handbag and even her phone. I guess inside her flat must be the same, because the front curtains are pink. She calls herself 'Pinky'.

No.43

The man in this house is tall and hefty but a sluggish mover — shoulders bent as he ambles along. Once, when he was a kid, I noticed out the window that he and some other kids were playing Knock Up Ginger in the street. As he reached our house I jerked open the front door at the same time as he pressed the bell. He jumped back, turned red, said something and ran off.

No.59

Each Sunday in the summer, a painter and decorator from farther up the street would put on his cricket whites and go off to play for his team. But one day he was stabbed in a fight, limped home with blood all over his leg and that was the end of his season.

No.65

Also at that end of the street lived an elderly woman who used to lay out dead bodies for people. Always wearing a black hat and coat, she smiled at everyone as she walked along, swaying from side to side.

No.69

Every morning a woman and her parents walk to the High Street and back from this house. They move briskly, leaning forward as though into a wind, the daughter way out in front. The man wears a khaki forage cap and carries a rucksack over one shoulder. Both the women have long straight hair, the mother's white and the daughter's mousy. The daughter is fatter than the parents and wears thick-lensed glasses, very unusual clothes and has prominent buck teeth. They are always together and never smile. The parents talk to each but the daughter stays silent. When they return, they never seem to be carrying shopping. They moved into their house when a relative left it to them. He was a cheerful old man and every day he'd walk very slowly backwards and forwards to the betting shop.

No.71

The little girl who lived here with her parents died, aged about nine, when a car hit her in the street outside the house. Afterwards the mother became stranger and stranger, accusing neighbours of attacking her. Then the father moved out, leaving her with another daughter. Occasionally social workers and police came to the house until one day, when she wouldn't answer the door, the police broke in and led her away in handcuffs, never to be seen again.

No.74

On this side of the street, at the far end, lived a tall fair-haired man who was the only person round here ever to display a Conservative Party election poster in his window. One evening he and his girlfriend had just walked out of his house when two youths stopped them, put a knife to her throat and demanded money, which he handed over. Soon afterwards he moved away.

No.68

The front garden is full of odds and ends. For years the West Indian woman who lives here has run a junk shop on the main street. She doesn't seem to have aged in all that time, but the other day, when I was out at the front of the house and she stopped to ask if she could take some lengths of wood that were stacked there, I noticed her greying afro and thought perhaps she did look older. Never having been in her shop, I hadn't spoken to her before, but I grew uncomfortable when she started accusing her next-door neighbour of abandoning her pets by shooing her cats and dogs out of her house and not letting them back in again. Not really believing this story, I at first tried to protest the woman's innocence, but she insisted it was true and so I let her ramble on until I excused myself and went back indoors.

A man used to work for her, or perhaps they ran the shop together. He'd walk around the streets pushing a metal trolley full of stuff. He was always bent double, his back at right angles to his legs. It looked painful and I haven't seen him for a long time.

No.62

This is where a couple and their son lived. Although I didn't want to hear it, the mother once told me that he used to wet the bed. As time passed, the father died, the mother went into a nursing home and the son was left living in the house on his own. The house deteriorated and I never saw the son around, though someone told me that he worked as a postman for a while. Then, years later, he reappeared, looking exactly like his father - his white hair and beard making him seem twenty or thirty years older than he must have been. Every day he walked to and from the shops, wearing shorts whatever the weather, winter or summer.

No.58

The fig tree planted in the front garden here has grown so big that its branches cover all the windows of this house and are starting to cover next door's too.

No.54

A woman lived here with her mother. When the mother died the woman's tall thin girlfriend moved in and the couple was together there for some years until the girlfriend suddenly moved out. The woman then started dating the vicar from the church at the end of the street, a short man with a bouffant hairstyle. They got married, she went to live with him and she sold the house.

No.52

Next door lived an Irish couple with their seven children – three boys and four girls. The father was a plasterer, although he was allergic to plaster. When some of the children got married and the parents moved back to Ireland with the youngest daughter, that left two sons and a daughter and her husband in the house. One of the sons would often come home in the middle of the night and play Elvis records very loud. The daughter and her husband had a stormy relationship and, when, she left him for good, her brothers soon went too. The husband was now alone in the house, though one or two women did stay briefly, but in the end the bank repossessed the house. The morning of the day that the people who bought the house were due to move in, he threw his remaining furniture over the back garden wall.

No.46

A lad who lives here has always dressed very stylishly. When he was younger he had the habit of, every few steps, spinning around a couple of times as he walked along the pavement. He doesn't seem to do it now.

No.36

Once, when a VW badge hanging round your neck was a popular hip-hop accessory, I glanced out of the window and saw a teenage girl who lived here starting to prise the Renault badge off the front of my car with a screwdriver. Perhaps she couldn't find a VW car nearby, or all their badges had been removed or she was thinking of a variation on the craze. When I opened my door she tucked the screwdriver up her sleeve and, when I accused her, she just shrugged. 'What am I supposed to be doing it with?' she asked. 'With the screwdriver up your sleeve,' I replied. She flushed and walked away. When she grew up she became a nurse.

No.26

Loud arguments regularly came from the house a couple of doors away from me when a family of six lived there – an Irish couple with three daughters and a son. The middle daughter and her boyfriend would have screaming rows in the street, usually finishing with him driving off in his white van. After the two elder sisters married – neither of them to the white van man - and moved away, both their parents and their brother died in the same year. The father, a friendly, quiet man with wavy white hair and recently retired from his road-sweeping job with the council, was the first to go, leaving the mother, the son and the youngest daughter in the house. The son became a drug addict and arguments between him and his mother grew more and more extreme. He communicated with his dealer by whistling out of his bedroom window. Sometimes he'd drag his girlfriend, a skinny, unhappy-looking girl, along the pavement by her hair. A hit-and-run driver, who was never caught, killed him one night. Soon afterwards the mother died. Now just the one daughter remains in the house. She is very shy.

No.12

One day I came home to find a back window broken in and things stolen. The usual stuff: TV, camera, cash. When the police came I told them I was suspicious of a couple of youths who lived towards the end of the street that I'd noticed hanging around eyeing up different houses. A few days later, after I'd just finished filling in an insurance claim form, the police phoned to tell me that all my stuff had been found, together with a lot of other people's, in the house of one of the youths. 'It was like Aladdin's cave in there,' said the policeman.

No.10

A teacher and his wife lived next door with their three children. The eldest son practised playing the flute in his bedroom. The kitchen, upstairs at the back of the house, had no ceiling and they'd placed basins on the rafters to catch drips from the leaky roof. When it rained the wife would stand at the sink singing 'Raindrops keep falling on my head'. They owned an ugly black cat that they called Lucky. It had very big balls and used to spray in our garden. The family once appeared on a TV quiz programme called *Ask the Family*. I can't remember how they got on.

No.4

When this house was empty and boarded up for a long time, a bag lady made its front porch her home. She'd stand there smiling for hours, like a soldier in a sentry box, surrounded by plastic carrier bags full of stuff.

Martyrs' Days

January 5

Yvonne's partner, back from the pub, smacks their puppy after it makes a mess on the floor. This starts an argument between him and Yvonne and, at his suggestion that she should go back to her mother's, she phones her son to come and pick her up. He sits down to eat his dinner in front of the TV and, when she grabs a piece of broccoli from his plate and throws it at him, he stands up and lashes out at her with his cutlery knife which sinks eight inches into her chest, penetrating both lungs. When Yvonne's son turns up at the flat in Britannia Close, her partner, covered in blood, refuses to let him in and leaves him waiting outside while he calls his own son who, when he arrives, tries to give Yvonne first aid. He cannot stem the flow of blood and she dies soon after being taken to hospital.

Tribal violence erupts in Kenya after the disputed presidential election between Raila Odinga, of the Orange Democratic Movement, and incumbent president Mwai Kibaki. Across the country, more than 800 people die in violence, mostly directed against the Kikuyu people.

A little girl, with braided hair and wearing a white Minnie Mouse top, jumps up and down, clapping her hands and shouting and singing. Her mother, phone to her ear and pushing twins in a buggy, follows her along the pavement.

Romanos walks into the bazaar in Constantinople with a dog tied to his belt. When people ask him why he is doing this he replies: 'To feed him as the Christians feed you Turks.' People grab him and take him before the Vizier and, when he repeats the same words, the Vizier orders that he be tortured until he denies his faith. They throw him into a dry well where he remains for forty days without food. Then they take him out and torture him further, but he still refuses to submit and the Vizier orders his beheading. They pass a mosque on the way to the place of execution and Romanos spits at it, whereupon the executioners cut out his tongue. When they behead him his body falls towards the east and lies there for three days and nights, lit by a heavenly light.

February 27

Solomon receives a phone call and tells his girlfriend he is going out for a short while. He is carrying £200 in cash and three one-ounce wraps of cocaine worth a total of £8,000. 40 minutes later, the man he has been speaking to on the phone attacks him, stealing one of the cocaine wraps and £140 of the cash and then stabbing him through the heart with a 10 cm blade. 'Help, I'm being robbed', shouts Solomon. The attacker runs off and Solomon tries to follow, shouting: 'Come on then, well you've stabbed me, so come on then, let's have it', before collapsing. Paramedics find him lying on the ground in Tilson Gardens and give him emergency treatment, but he dies there an hour later.

The Somali government's operation against Al-Shabab militants results in the deaths of 115 people: 49 civilians, 60 militants and six African Union peacekeepers as well as 157 people wounded.

An African man, dressed all in black and wearing a black baseball cap, shouts up and gestures at a first floor balcony of the red brick block of flats. A woman appears between the two clothes rails full of drying laundry. She throws down a pink child's satchel which he catches and limps away with.

They take Anne from Newgate Prison for trial at the Old Bailey. She is so weak from fever that they carry her in a chair into the courtroom where the judge sentences her to death by hanging for the crime of assisting a priest. On the scaffold she declares loudly to the watching crowd: 'I am sentenced to die for harbouring a Catholic priest, and so far I am from repenting for having so done, that I wish, with all my soul, that where I have entertained one, I could have entertained a thousand.'

March 2

Two members of the TN1 (Trust No One) gang spot Kwame and his friend walking through the Moorlands Estate and chase them into Adelaide Close. His friend manages to escape by climbing over a wall, but Kwame is trapped and dies after the gang knife him 14 times in the back.

A suicide bomber kills 23 people in an attack on the headquarters of the Lashkar-e-Islam group in the Tirah Valley region of northwest Pakistan close to the border with Afghanistan, where clashes earlier in the day between Pakistani security forces and militants kill seven troops and 20 insurgents from an unknown group.

A fat woman, a spider web tattoo covering her shaven head, pushes a baby along in a buggy. A youth, bright green hair coming out of part of his head in a long tuft, walks beside her.

During the famine in Flanders, Count Charles distributes bread to the poor and, to prevent grain from being hoarded and sold at excessively high prices by the Erembald family, starts proceedings to reduce that family to the status of serfs. As a result, Bertulf FitzErembald, provost of the church of St. Donatian, in Bruges, conspires to assassinate Charles and his advisors. On the morning of March 2, as Charles kneels in prayer in that church, knights answering to the Erembald family enter the building and hack him to death with broadswords.

April 17

When two men in the Brixton McDonald's queue start arguing, Devon asks them to 'calm down and behave'. Another man, who has not been involved in the argument, objects to this and squares up to Devon in front of security guards who then throw him and Devon out. They continue their argument in the street and, when people try to intervene, the man tells them that Devon has been 'too disrespectful', is going to be 'shot in the head' and will be 'filled up with lead'. They agree to meet in a nearby street. The man phones a friend and asks him to join him and to bring a gun. The two men find Devon and chase him into Marcus Garvey Way. The man's friend shouts: 'Shoot him, shoot him', and Devon says: 'Oh my God, he's got a gun, he's going to shoot me'. The man fires three shots at Devon at close range and two hit him. Devon remains on his feet at first but they push him to the ground, kick him, punch him in the face and hit him on the head with the gun. 'You're not so hot now', says the man before the two of them walk away. Neighbours come out of their homes to find Devon lying bleeding on the ground, holding his stomach and saying: 'He shot me'. He is taken to hospital for emergency surgery but dies a few hours later. A post-mortem examination reveals one bullet damaged the left femoral artery in his thigh near his groin and the other passed through his intestine.

The Mexican Navy captures the leader of a drug cartel involved in the massacre of 145 people found buried in a mass grave near the US border. Martin Omar Estrada Luna ('El Kilo') is the head of the Zetas gang which is behind the killing of 72 Central and South American migrants in the same area where the 145 bodies were recovered.

A short, elderly woman with long straggly hair passes by. In one hand she carries a walking stick and in the other she swings a birdcage with two budgerigars inside, swaying back and forth on their perch.

A wealthy woman, who grazes her sheep and cattle on the island of Eigg, resents the presence of Donnan and his monks and persuades a band of sea robbers to murder them. The pirates come to the church where Donnan is celebrating Holy Communion. They allow him to finish the service and afterwards the celebrants go to the refectory, Donnan having told them: 'We may not die, so long as we remain in the joy of the Lord. However, let us go where we refresh our bodies and there pay the mortal penalty.' The pirates then set the refectory on fire and 52 perish in the flames or by the sword, Donnan himself being beheaded.

May 4

Alim meets the boy at Tilford House on Holmewood Gardens to collect the bike that he bought from him at school for £90. The boy demands £50 more and an argument starts. Some of the boy's friends appear, drag Alim up to the top-floor walkway of the flats and stab him seven times in his arms, legs and chest. A resident finds him covered in blood and dust, calls the emergency services and tries to resuscitate him until paramedics arrive. They take him to hospital where, with his parents at his bedside, he dies.

Militants attack a bus of Shiite pilgrims to the north of Baghdad, killing 11 people and wounding 21. To the south of the city, they shoot dead a family of eight.

Two caretakers: one wears a fluorescent yellow waistcoat and carries a spade and a bag of rubbish; the other, with a pair of gloves sticking out of one back pocket of his overalls and a cleaning rag sticking out of the other, carries a bucket in one hand and a mop with a dustpan attached in the other. Pigeons pecking at the grass ignore them while a thrush perched on a lamppost looks down at them.

Emperor Diocletian, captivated by Pelagia's beauty, promises her great riches if she rejects Christianity and becomes his wife. She refuses his offer, telling him: 'You are insane, Emperor, saying such things to me. I will not do your bidding, and I loathe your vile marriage, since I have Christ, the king of heaven, as my bridegroom. I do not desire your worldly crown which lasts only a short while. The Lord in his heavenly kingdom has prepared three imperishable crowns for me. The first is for faith, since I have believed in the true God with all my heart; the second is for purity, because I have dedicated my virginity to him; the third is for martyrdom, since I want to accept every suffering for him and offer up my soul because of my love for him.' Diocletian sentences her to be burned in a red-hot bronze bull. Not allowing the executioners to touch her body, she makes the sign of the cross and steps into the bull. When her flesh melts, a myrrh-like fragrance fills the whole city of Rome, but her bones remain unharmed and are removed to a place outside the city. Four lions then come out of the wilderness and sit around the bones, protecting them until

Bishop Linus of Tarsus comes to gather them up and bury them.

June 17

After Czarina argues with her partner in front of their six month-old daughter about his failure to help around the house, he throttles her with the straps of a nappy bag while forcing her head into a bowl full of water used to cool the baby's bottle. He then attempts suicide by taking 40 sleeping pills and drinking white spirits, detergent and limescale remover. That being ineffective, he tries to hang himself and then sits for hours with a live cable in a bath of water. Three days later he walks into a police station and confesses to the killing. When detectives go to the flat in Hemans Street, they find Czarina's dead body wrapped in a sleeping bag underneath a quilt.

Street fighting between ethnic Kyrgyz and minority Uzbeks escalates in the city of Osh, Kyrgyzstan, leaving at least 200 people dead. Uzbek neighbourhoods are torched, displacing thousands of people and approximately 100,000 cross the border into Uzbekistan.

An ambulance drives up and stops. Two paramedics get out, one holding a cool box and the other a plastic container and a fork. They cross the road to another ambulance already parked in the road and join two other paramedics sitting in the back of this ambulance with its side door wide open. The four of them then eat their lunch from various containers. Afterwards, the one the cool box takes out a jar of coffee, a pint of milk, a thermos flask of hot water and four mugs and makes coffee for everyone.

The Persian emperor sends the brothers Manuel, Sabel and Ismael as emissaries to conclude a peace treaty with the Roman emperor Julian who receives them honourably at Chalcedon. But when the brothers refuse to take part in a sacrifice to the Roman gods, Julian tells them that if they scorn the gods he worships, it will be impossible to reach any peace or accord between the two empires. The brothers reply that they have been sent as emissaries of their emperor on matters of state, and not to argue about gods. Julian then annuls the treaty, imprisons the brothers and orders them to be tortured. The torturers beat the brothers, and then nail their hands and feet to trees. Later, they drive iron spikes into their heads, and wedge sharp splinters under their fingernails and toenails. Finally, they behead them. Julian orders their bodies to be burned, and suddenly there is an earthquake. The ground opens up and the brothers' bodies disappear into the ground. After two days the earth return the bodies from which a sweet fragrance issues forth. Many people, witnessing the miracle, come to believe in Christ and are baptized.

July 27

After Simon spends the day drinking with his girlfriend, his drug dealer and a Japanese woman, they return to the girlfriend's flat in Edgington Road, buying wine at an off-licence on the way. The dealer offers to supply them with cocaine and, when he sells the girlfriend an ecstasy pill, Simon becomes annoyed and an argument starts in the kitchen that continues after the women go to bed drunk. Neighbours hear Simon saying: 'So you have a knife - are you going to stab me?' and then: 'Fuck off and get out,' to which the dealer replies: 'I'm going to stab you. You are a dead man.' The dealer goes home, collects a knife and returns. He stabs Simon in the arm and twice in the abdomen, damaging the major artery leading from his heart, and then leaves. At 3.30am the girlfriend finds Simon lying in a pool of blood in the kitchen. Her screams wake neighbours who call an ambulance, but the injuries prove fatal.

After Iran's Supreme Court approves the death sentences, 29 people are hanged at dawn in Evin Prison in Tehran, among them convicts found guilty of murder, rape, armed robbery and drug trafficking.

The man says a couple of words, gives a jerk to pull the small white dog away from the tree and then lets the lead extend. The dog looks up at his owner, shakes itself and then trots on ahead, wagging its tail. When the dog sniffs at something in the gutter the owner stops and swops the lead over to his other hand.

Titus's fight against the spread of Nazi ideology and for educational and press freedom in Holland leads the German occupiers to arrest him at the Boxmeer monastery and take him to a prison at Scheveningen. His interrogator asks: 'Why have you disobeyed the regulations?' Titus replies: 'As a Catholic, I could have done nothing differently. We must object to anything or any philosophy that is not in line with Catholic doctrine.' After transfers to prisons at Amersfoort and Kleve, Titus is sent to the Dachau concentration camp where his calmness and gentleness infuriates the guards who regularly kick him and beat him with fists and clubs, often leaving him nearly unconscious. His health gives way and, in the camp hospital, an SS doctor gives him a lethal injection as part of the program of medical experimentation on the prisoners.

August 1

After DJing at Club Life, Carl leaves the club with his friends. As they walk along Goding Street towards their car, a group of 11 men approaches them. After an argument between one of the men and one of Carl's friends, a fight breaks out during which Carl is stabbed. His friends put him in the car and drive to a hospital, but police stop the car when it runs through a red light. They discover Carl seriously hurt and call for an ambulance. Despite emergency surgery, he dies.

A masked man, dressed in black, interrupts 'Youth get together', a weekly event for gay youths held in the basement of a building in Tel-Aviv in Israel and opens fire on the crowd with a pistol. The room is small, preventing anyone from escaping, and people hide under a bed and tables, but the gunman kills two people, wounds 15 and then leaves.

The two minicab drivers half-sit on their cab bonnets. One smokes and the other drinks from a can. The smoker points out a fox walking along the pavement opposite. The drinker laughs and throws his can at the animal, but it misses and the fox stops, looks at the men and walks on.

After killing or deporting the Jewish population of Navahrudak, the Nazi authorities begin executing and arresting Polish inhabitants and suspected partisans. When more than 120 people are arrested and slated for execution, eleven Sisters of the Holy Family of Nazareth offer their lives in exchange for the imprisoned and the Nazis instead deport the prisoners to work camps in Germany. When the life of their chaplain is threatened, the nuns renew their offer. Without warning the Nazis imprison the nuns, load them into a van, drive them to woods outside the town where they shoot them and bury them in a common grave.

September 27

Junior is playing football with friends on the grass outside the block of flats where he lives on the Loughborough Estate when a group of girls approaches. An argument starts and one of the girls goes back to her home and returns with a knife. When one of her friends takes the knife away from her, she contacts her boyfriend and, later that evening, in a street on the estate, he stabs Junior. Reports of the incident bring police, paramedics and the air ambulance to the scene where they pronounce Junior dead.

A bomb placed outside a courthouse in Yemen's Hadramout province explodes, killing three children when one of them steps on the bomb as they walk along the street.

A workman pushes a wheelbarrow full of safety helmets past a little boy trying not to step on the cracks between the paving stones.

One of Callistratus's fellow soldiers overhears him praying to Christ and reports this to General Persesntinian, the military commander in Rome, who summons Callistratus and orders him to offer sacrifice to the gods. When he refuses, he is beaten, dragged over stones, sewn into a leather sack and thrown into the sea. The sack strikes a sharp rock, tears open and dolphins carry Callistratus to dry land unharmed. When the soldiers see this miracle, and 49 of them convert to Christ, the military commander orders Callistratus and the converted soldiers to be flogged, bound hand and foot and thrown into a dam. But their bonds break, and they stand in the water, rejoicing in their baptism. Beautiful bright crowns appear over their heads, and all hear a voice: 'Be brave, Callistratus, with your company, and come rest in the eternal habitations.' At the same time, the earth shudders and a statue of a Roman god standing nearby falls down and smashes. Seeing this, another 135 soldiers also declare for Christ. The military commander, fearing a mutiny in the army, orders all the believers to be cut to pieces with swords.

October 25

Two men knock on the door of Luthan's ninth floor flat in Nevil House and ask to buy cannabis. He lets them in and starts cutting the drug with a kitchen knife. When one of the men shouts: 'Give me all the money and give me all the herb,' Luthan, still carrying the knife, runs into his bedroom, where his girlfriend is asleep. The men pursue him and one of them wrestles the knife from him and uses it to stab him, while the other one, after punching Luthan in the face, picks up the ice cream tub containing the stash of cannabis and says: 'Let's go.' Luthan tells his girlfriend to hand over his wallet to his attackers, but they are unhappy with its contents and stab him in the back a final time before leaving with 500g of cannabis and £100 cash. The girlfriend calls the emergency services and when they arrive they rush Luthan to hospital where he dies of his wounds, having been stabbed three times in the back – one blow piercing a lung – twice in the arm and once in the chest, with the knife slicing through a rib.

Pro-government Arab militias attack rebel-held villages in the area of Muhajiriya, east of the South Darfur capital, Nyala, burning homes and stealing livestock. The fighting kills more than 40 civilians and displaces about 12,000, many of them sheltering under trees and lacking basic supplies of food and water.

Three small boys, dressed completely in Chelsea football kit, wait to cross the road with their father. A man wearing a black 'Judgement Hour' t-shirt and enormous headphones glances at them as he walks past.

A 400-strong crowd, led by the Vicar of Leigh, surrounds Father Ambrose and his congregation at Morleys Hall in Astley. Ambrose surrenders and the others are released after their names have been recorded. They take the partially paralysed priest to Lancaster Castle. When Ambrose appears before the judge at his trial, he professes his adherence to the Catholic faith, defends his actions and is found guilty and sentenced to be executed. Two days later, he is drawn on a hurdle to the scaffold, hanged, dismembered, quartered, and boiled in oil. Afterwards the executioners display his head on a pike.

November 13

While he is out of town, the man who runs a telephone drug-dealing service tells Leroy to mind his drugs and phones. When he returns, he suspects Leroy of using the supply instead of selling it, so he and another man visit Leroy at his maisonette in Crichton Street and shoot him twice in the head with a shotgun. They ask another man to cover up the killing by starting a fire. But he uses so much petrol - two can-loads – that he causes an explosion that blows up the entire house. When fire fighters extinguish the fire they find Leroy's body.

Mistaking it for a merchant ship, Somali pirates in a speedboat attack a Kenyan naval patrol boat off the coastal town of Kilifi in the India Ocean. When four of the pirates board the patrol boat, Kenyan navy officers shoot dead three of them while the wounded fourth one dives into the sea.

The woman comes out of her front door and lights up a cigarette. She steps over the weeds growing up from the cracks in the kerbstones and pushes an overhanging bush away from the path, pressing it into the fence. She puts a phone to her ear and walks into the park where starlings peck amongst the grass.

Disguised as a sailor, Damascene, a monk from Constantinople, goes to the Ayasofya mosque and proclaims Christ as the true God. The worshippers ignore him and he goes to the Sultan Mehmed mosque and repeats his proclamation, calling the Moslems ignorant and deceived because they do not believe in Christ. But those who hear him think him insane. The next day Damascene goes to the vizier's courtyard and shouts at those he finds there: 'Your faith is not true. Christ is the true God, and only the faith of Christ is true.' They seize and beat him and chase him away. Then he goes to the Tophana mosque and again he is seized and beaten. This time, however, he is sent to the Grand Vizier. Seeing that Damascene will not convert to Islam, the Vizier sentences him to death before the gates of the Patriarchate. Thanking God for allowing him martyrdom, he kneels down, bends his neck and is beheaded.

December 2

Donald is helping out at Stockwell Park Community Centre when he gets into an argument with a group of youths, who then punch, kick and hit him with a chair. He is taken to hospital with head injuries where he remains in a critical condition until his death two weeks later.

During clashes in the Hadramout region of Yemen, militants attack an army checkpoint at the western entrance of the city of Sayoun, resulting in the deaths of three soldiers and six militants.

The tall, thin man with the greying ponytail smokes a cigarette as he skates around. Fraying shirt cuffs poke out beneath the sleeves of his black leather coat and half cover his fingerless gloves. His companion, a longhaired, bearded man, tries to jump up on his board onto the platform but falls over and lies there laughing. Then he walks away and later returns with a can of drink and something in a white paper bag.

Apronianus, Governor of Rome, orders the Christian sisters, Bibiana and Demetria, to be stripped of all their possessions and left to suffer poverty. They remain in their house, spending their time in fasting and prayer until Apronianus, seeing that hunger and want has no effect on them, summons them to appear before him. Demetria, after confessing her faith, falls dead at his feet while Bibiana is placed in the hands of Rufina, a wicked woman who tries to seduce her. Despite blows as well as persuasion, Bibiana remains chaste. Apronianus then orders her to be tied to a pillar and beaten with scourges until she dies. Her body is then left in the open to be torn apart by wild animals, yet none of them touch it and after two days she is buried.

To the River

As I leave the house, a car pulls up. The woman who's driving gets out, goes round to the passenger side, opens the door, pulls out a young girl and drags her by her hair across the road and into the house opposite. She comes back out to the car and spits into the gutter. Noticing me, she smiles and shrugs, but says nothing.

A hearse stops outside the Congregational School. It's more of a cart really - it badly needs repainting and the glass is all cracked. The driver gets down and fixes feed-bags over the horses' noses. A man comes out of the school doors, pushing through the usual group of smokers standing on the pavement, and stares at the hearse and then at the driver.

'What do you think you're doing?'

The driver continues adjusting the feed-bags and then looks round. 'Seeing to the horses.'

'Do you intend to remain here?'

'I've just come from the fever hospital up the road and I'm leaving this here while I go in and have a drink.' He points to the pub next door.

'You can't leave dead bodies in front of a school.'

'They're both in coffins – and anyway, what's it to you?'

'I'm the schoolmaster, and this is becoming too regular an occurrence. It's unhealthy, very distracting for the children and extremely disrespectful to leave the departed like that outside a public house. I'm going to write to the authorities.'

'As you wish,' says the driver as he strolls into the pub.

I notice a white van following close behind a black car

travelling slowly along Stockwell Road. When they stop at traffic lights the van driver leans out of his window and shouts: 'Why don't you get off the phone?' The car driver gets out, walks back to the van and punches the driver a few times in the face through the open window. He then returns to his car and, as the lights have changed to green, drives off, pursued by the van.

Waiting to cross the road outside The Swan, I glance at the posters outside the pub advertising the acts for the coming months - *Bondi Beach Bums* and *Evil Puppies* – and then I overhear three men having a conversation in the pub doorway. Two are very rough looking, with scarred unshaven faces, strange caps and patched coats, but the other is a thin, obviously very respectable gentleman, with a fine powdered wig, and elegant dark topcoat and tricorn hat.

'That was too close on the common last night. You might have lost that whole consignment. Who could have tipped off the authorities?'

'We'll find him. But we showed them anyway. I've never seen men run so fast.'

'Well no, they don't like being fired at. But perhaps be careful in the future. Murder is bad for business. And hanging would be bad for you too.'

'Pay no heed sir, we were only frightening them. Anyway, now it's safely stored in our warehouse, not far away, and when you're ready we'll deliver.'

'It hasn't to go far, just to Vauxhall Gardens. And I hope that it will be in good condition – I found that the last fellows I did business with were not to be trusted in that respect.'

'Oh no sir, it's all good stuff – and at a very fair price.'

'Well I hope you're right.'

A woman, I think she's African, with braided hair and wearing a long black leather coat, is standing outside the betting shop and chanting loudly. She's holding a bible in one hand whilst punching the air and gesturing with the other. Propped against her stomach is a white placard with a bible quotation printed on it. It's John 3:4-5: 'Nicodemus said to him…' I can't figure out what she's singing, just bits of phrases: 'He's so perfect, he's so good,' and 'Repent, repent, repent.' Passers-by ignore her, but one of them hands me a small printed card:

> *Professor* TOUBA
> *Clairvoyant. Medium and Africa Astrologer*
> A RECOMMENDED PROFESSIONAL SPIRITUAL
> HEALER FROM ANCESTORS.
> *Born gifted with spiritual power. No matter what your problems are.*
> GUARANTEE TO HELP YOU IN ANY PROBLEMS
> ARE JEALOUSY, VOODOO, UGANGA, BUSINESS,
> HEALTH, SEXUAL DIFFICULTIES,
> LEADERSHIPS, POPULARITY ETC. IF HUSBAND
> OR WIFE HAS WALKED OUT, I WILL BRING HIM
> OR HER BACK. I HAVE THE EXPERTISE AND
> KNOWLEDGE TO EXPLAIN THROUGH TAROT
> CARD, CRYSTAL BALL, PALM, CANDLE,
> PICTURE, DREAM AND TEA LEAF READINGS. I
> WILL WARN YOU GRAVELY, SUGGEST WISELY
> AND EXPLAIN FULLY.
> *I can also come to your House to see if there are any Evil Spirits*

As I walk past the Lidl supermarket, deep in thought from Professor Touba's message, A young man stops me. He doffs his hat, showing his wavy red hair

'Excuse me sir. Am I going in the right way to Dulwich?'

'Mm… yes. Are you walking all the way? It's over three miles, I think. You could take a a tram.'

'Oh no, I like to walk.'

I try to place his accent.

'Well, if you walk down this road you will come to Brixton. And then you should take the road to Herne Hill. Dulwich is a little farther on from there.'

'Thank you sir. I arrived in London recently. I am living along there.' He points up the Clapham Road. 'Hackford Road. Now I wish to visit the Picture Gallery at Dulwich.'

'I've heard that it's a nice gallery. And where are you from?'

'From Den Haag...in Holland. I work here in London ...I am very happy to be here.'

I look at his face and think that he doesn't look very happy.

'Well good luck, and I hope you enjoy your time here.'

'Thank you sir.'

He strides away from me, down towards Brixton, into the sun.

The traffic has become stationary and as I approach Oval Station I can see why. A mass of people is filling the whole street, cheering and laughing. Hawkers are busy selling all sorts of things: fruit, pies, sweetmeats, sheets of verses. I turn to a man who's standing on tiptoes, straining to get a view over the heads of the crowd.

'What's going on?' I ask.

'It's the new gallows they've set up on the corner of the common over there. Too far to Tyburn it seems. And now they're going to burn Sarah Elston - she murdered her husband you know. That's her, up over there...'

I can just see a young woman standing swaying on a rough wooden cart with two soldiers holding her upright. Her face is as white as her dress.

'And they're waiting for a couple of villains to swing as well – they're there too somewhere.'

Not wanting to have anything to do with all that stuff and the hymn singing and pickpocketing that goes with it, I squeeze on through the shouts and smells.

I walk through the flock of sheep grazing in the Oval. Outside the Durham Arms a couple of men seemingly not interested in watching the executions are swigging porter and exchanging words with a crossing-sweeper clearing away the horseshit in the middle of the road.

Cox's Bridge seems to be falling to pieces and I cross carefully, not wishing to fall into the sewer that the Effra's become. At the turnpike, both cyclists and pedestrians coming out of the station are ignoring red traffic lights.

Above the sound of the traffic I can hear music. It must be the Vauxhall Gardens orchestra rehearsing for the evening's entertainment. It sounds like *The Lass of Richmond Hill*, always one of my favourites. Someone leaves Chariot's, turns and curtsies to the man on the door. It's Princess Seraphina, wearing his usual white calamanco gown and scarlet cloak, with his hair frizzled and curled all round his forehead and fluttering a fan.

Finally reaching the Thames, I stand on Vauxhall Bridge, looking down at where the Effra reaches its end. Rubbish floats past, twisting in the brown green water on its way to the sea: scraps of plastic, wood and paper; contraceptives and orange peels. The MI6 building looms over me, a ziggurat of spiked railings, cream and green stacks, CCTV cameras, hoists and satellite dishes.

I hear faint shouts from the north side of the river. I can just make out a line of convicts in front of the long grey walls of the prison. Weighed down with chains, they're shuffling down steps from the embankment and across a gangplank to a boat moored there. Warders, who seem to be the ones doing the shouting, wave their guns at the convicts.

'Transportation.'

I turn my head. I hadn't noticed a man joining me, leaning on the side of the bridge. He looks just like Larry David.

'They're taking them down to the convict ships moored downriver. Then off to Australia with them.'

'A long way.'

'Better than the drop.'

'I suppose you're right.'

'Poms, they call them there.'

'Poms?'

He grins. 'Prisoners of Millbank.'

Fitzrovia Junctures

The man in the fluorescent yellow waistcoat drops one of the lengths of piping that he's carrying through the front door of 58 Grafton Way. 'Careful with those,' says the foreman. 'And keep the racket down. Those foreigners are having a meeting upstairs. Organizing the liberation of Venezuela, they told me. So they want less noise.'

Six workmen, eating sandwiches and drinking from paper cups, are sitting on the pavement with their backs leaning against Fitzroy Square's garden railings. One of them whistles when Virginia Woolf walks past. The others laugh. 'You've got to be joking, mate,' says the shaven-headed one. 'Much too skinny. And she don't look all there, either.'

The Westminster Council lorry waits in the square while one of the recycling team brings three plastic sacks up from the basement of number 29, unaware that one of the sacks contains the discarded drafts for *Arms and the Man*. Upstairs, George Bernard Shaw strokes his beard, his pen poised.

Sir Charles Eastlake hesitates before he gets into the hansom cab outside number 7 and looks up at the front of the house. He turns to a workman in a yellow safety helmet who's leaning against the railings and smoking a cigarette. 'Do you have any idea how much longer this scaffolding is due to stay up?'

The workman turns to him and shrugs. "No idea mate. Best to ring head office.'

Sir Charles sighs. 'National Gallery,' he tells the driver as he climbs into the cab.

The Marquess of Salisbury turns to his wife. 'Do you realize, Georgina, that there's a group of people down there letting their dogs jump through the railings and tear about in the garden. And look, one of those animals is cocking his leg up against the Barbara Hepworth. I just don't know what this square is coming to.'

'Really, my dear?'

'And now there's a man, in some sort of uniform, standing in front of our car writing something down. He looks like an African. Do you think he's anything to do with those Mozambique people downstairs?'

'That must be a traffic warden. I believe they call them Civil Enforcement Officers now. Your driver must have parked on a double yellow line again. I expect you'll be receiving another fine.'

'That's absurd. Don't they realize I'm the Prime Minister?'

Returning to his lodgings in Cleveland Street, Samuel Morse sees a notice pinned to the front door. He leans forward to examine it more closely, tapping his fingers on the door in annoyance as he reads that Vinyasa yoga classes are to be held every Thursday in the All Souls Clubhouse that occupies the ground floor and basement of the building. When one of the club members appears, he points at the notice. 'This is disgraceful,' he tells her furiously. 'To allow such heathen practices in a Christian house.'

When James Boswell wakes up with a bad hangover, he shouts for his manservant. 'Francis, is the Horse and Groom open yet?'

'No sir, it doesn't open until midday.'

'Well, are there any whores about in the street?'

'It's still rather early for them too sir.'

'Then go over to Greggs and bring me back one of their breakfast deals. How much are they?'

'£2.25, sir.'

'Well then, get me two.'

There's a loud crash and Ed Murrow looks up from his typewriter. 'Oh God,' says his wife. 'Have the Germans finally started bombing?'

He walks over to the window, looks out and shakes his head. 'No honey, it's only some truck delivering beer to the Masons Arms next door.' He lights up another Camel. 'And anyhow, while the scaffolding is up this building is protected by Cactus Security.'

The car bringing John Reith back from a meeting with the Prime Minister about the abdication crisis stops outside the BBC headquarters. Reith remains for a while in the back seat, looking with disgust at his various employees lounging around outside on Portland Place, some in t-shirts, others wearing jeans and trainers. He sighs angrily at the sight of a young woman in shorts in the arms of an unshaven man. 'What is that thing he's wearing on his head?' he asks his driver.

'I believe it's called a baseball cap, sir,' the driver replies.

From his studio above Domino's Pizza, Henry Fuseli, brush in hand, stares down at the contrasts of light and dark caused by the streetlight shining on the man sitting on the pavement opposite. The man, with matted long blond hair and wearing a dirty black duffle coat, is eating a discarded piece of pizza. He appears to notice Fuseli's attention and gets to his feet, picks up his bulging orange plastic bags and walks slowly up Hanson Street, still chewing.

Saki walks into the offices of the Artemis recruitment agency where a woman at the reception desk is peering into a computer. 'Good morning,' he says, smoothing down his brilliantined hair, 'I'm looking for a personal secretary.'

She looks up. 'Very well sir. Do you have any specific requirements?'

'Yes. Must be a man. A youngish, personable-looking man. And not Jewish. My name's Munro. I work at home, just round the corner in Mortimer Street.'

The barman in The King and Queen looks Bob Dylan up and down and nods at his guitar. 'You've got the wrong night, son. Friday night is the folk club.' He points at the large TV screen up on the wall. 'It's Premier League football tonight. Arsenal v Chelsea, if you're interested.' Bob shakes his head and walks out into the freezing evening, past the thumping bass coming from the delivery van parked in the street.

Thumbing his smartphone, the bored driver sits in the black Mercedes parked outside 49 Tottenham Street. Inside, after the talk by Keir Hardie, the mood in the Communist Club is turning unpleasant. 'This organization is getting more and more bourgeois,' shouts one member. 'One minute we find that a burglar alarm has been installed and now, if you care to look outside, there's a large expensive car with a chauffeur waiting to collect someone here.'

'Well comrade,' says Hardie, 'that chauffeur *is* a worker. Would it make you happier if he got a ticket?'

The black guy with the Mohican haircut walks along Goodge Street. He's wearing a *Night of the Living Dead* t-shirt, carrying a red shoulder bag and his green earrings match his green tracksuit bottoms. Roger Fry turns his head to stare as he passes and nearly drops the pot he's carrying.

Because John Constable is strolling along gazing up at the clouds rather than looking where he's going, he bumps headlong into Robert Smirke, the architect who lives just down the road from him.

'Why don't you have a look at the exhibition in that Woolff Gallery opposite you?' says Smirke, after they make their apologies. 'You might find it interesting. The artist has made all these pieces using old record labels he's collected – Tamla, Sex Pistols, Elvis and so on.'

'It doesn't sound my sort of thing,' says Constable.

When the Fifth Congress is adjourned for the day, Vladimir Lenin and Josef Stalin leave the hall and walk down Charlotte Street, discussing the failings of the Mensheviks and the need to build a revolutionary working class party. They stop outside the Fitzroy Tavern and look at the menu displayed outside.

'What is Chicken Achari?' asks Lenin.

Stalin shrugs. 'I've no idea. Shall we try the Mega Sharing Platter?'

'Very well. And look, they take Visa cards.'

At closing time George Orwell and a fellow Home Guard sergeant leave the Newman Arms. 'How will you get home?' asks Orwell.

The sergeant nods towards the cycle docking station. 'I'll use one of those Boris bikes.'

Orwell shakes his head. 'I don't think you should call them that, nor ride one.'

'Really? Why not?'

'Firstly because the original idea was Livingstone's and secondly because Johnson is a frightful reactionary. So, one has to get one's facts right and also stick to one's principles.'

Aleister Crowley and Dylan Thomas stagger out of the Marquis of Granby and Crowley points at the Buca Lounge opposite. 'Now for shisha.'

Thomas looks puzzled. 'What?'

'You know. Hookah pipe… Hubble bubble. I used them in North Africa.'

They cross the road but the Buca Lounge's door is locked and its windows are covered in photocopied notices:

> TO WHOM IT MAY CONCERN
> THE ESPRESSO COFFEE MACHINE, GRINDER, KNOCK BOX AND WATER TREATMENT UNIT ARE THE PROPERTY OF UK COOLING SOLUTIONS LTD. WE WANT THESE RETURNED. WE REQUIRE ACCESS TO REMOVE OUR GOODS FROM SITE. RUSLAN, PLEASE CALL US TO RETURN OUR GOODS

'I think the place is closed,' says Thomas.

Augustus John studies the Protape shop window. Charles Laughton, whose flat is above the shop, has arranged to meet him there so that they can walk down to the Apollo Theatre together. 'What are all these things?' asks John when Laughton appears.

'They're external drives. Elsa thinks we should get one to keep copies of our films and publicity photos on.'

John tugs at his moustache. 'Hm…Could I keep copies of my paintings and drawings on one?'

'Yes, but you'd have to get a PC first.'

The emergency response cars, lights flashing, drive past the Crossrail construction works into Stephen's Mews. Policemen pile out of their cars and start to batter down the door and windows of number 7, where a meeting of German anarchists is taking place at the International Club. When the members open the door and see not only police but also a large crowd of angry onlookers, they appeal to the police for protection. 'We'll protect you damned foreigners with the staff,' a sergeant replies and both police and the crowd charge into the club, wounding some of the members and carrying off jars of beer, papers, books, money and even some of the members' clothes.

Voyage

Lean against wall, hands in pockets. Cough into chest. Cough again, louder.

Fold canvas over and over. Stamp flat with right foot. Put arms above head and stretch back. Look around.

Shift from foot to foot. Spit into drain and walk up alleyway, swaying from side to side.

Bend over rail, holding stomach. Spew up. Wipe mouth with forearm. Spit and wipe mouth again.

Pick up cigarette end from gutter. Cross square. Pause in front of supermarket and ask men for money.

Slide zigzagging along deck. Grab and hold rail. Pick splinter from palm.

Stop outside off-licence, jingling coins in pocket. Take out coins and look at them.

Lick wound. Take rag from pocket and dab at blood. Throw rag into sea. Go below.

Enter off-licence and come out carrying can of beer. Cross road, drinking from can.

Ease line through fingers, counting. Curse loudly and jump to one side.

Sit down in doorway. Take packet of biscuits from carrier-bag and eat one after the other, chewing hard.

Untie knot. Wrap twine round and round thumb and forefinger. Drop down onto right knee.

Get up from doorway, waving stick at pigeons. Walk round in circles on pavement, picking at teeth.

Climb up ladder, rung by rung. Pause and brush spray from front of jacket. Continue ascent.

Take cigarette packet from litter-bin and drop it back in again. Walk through square, looking into every bin.

Tug at bits of old rope, slowly untangling. Look up at sky. Blow into clenched fists.

Pull newspaper from litter-bin. Glance at headlines and read back page. Fold and put into coat pocket.

Haul on rope, hand over hand. Stagger against wind. Trip over plank and fall down. Lie groaning.

Stand staring in middle of road. Hitch up trousers. Scratch inside shirt. Shake head up and down.

Run down steps. Empty contents of bucket over rail. Look down at waves. Walk astern.

Place carrier-bag against bus stop. Hold out hand to passer-by. Shout out something.

Scrape at deck, back and forth. Sit back on heels and rub sweat from forehead.

Look into shop window and stamp foot. Talk to woman sweeping steps. Walk away, laughing.

Stand on tiptoes, holding hand up before face. Screw up eyes. Point at horizon. Run to starboard.

Leaving

Stopping for a minute to peer into the hallway mirror and prod at the wrinkles around my eyes, I step out of the front door and slam it shut behind me.

I see that they've taken the scaffolding down from a house across the road, but they've left a pile of timber out on the pavement. All the houses round here are two-storey, terraced jobs, built in the early 1870s. The house directly opposite mine has a white burglar alarm on the wall, but I've never heard it go off – it's probably a fake; the paint on its window frames peeled off some time ago; the front yard wall is built of breeze blocks painted pink, chunks of which have flaked away and behind this wall is a privet hedge – rarely trimmed. On the rare occasions the owner decides to cut the hedge he uses an ordinary pair of household scissors, so it can take him a couple of days.

Three elderly West Indian women are walking towards me. They're dressed like women from the 1950s, with brimmed hats and long overcoats and, because of their size and their age, they walk very slowly, swaying from side to side. I know that they want to talk to me about 'The Bible' or 'The End of the World', because groups of women like these appear in the street regularly, perhaps twice a week. It doesn't make sense – they always come round during the day when most people are at work. If their churches got younger, more agile people to go round the houses faster, and in the evening, then perhaps they could convert more, if that's what they want to do. Usually I ignore the bell when they call, even though they stand on the doorstep for a long time after ringing it. But if I answer the door by mistake or if, like now, they catch me outside, I never say anything, just smile and shake my head so that they might think I'm foreign and don't understand English. This is what I do now, but I realise they've heard me talking to myself so I nod and take the leaflet one of them hands me. I glance at it – it's something to do with the end of the world.

I walk down the street, past the orange rubbish sacks along the pavement and the new 'For Sale' signs that have appeared. Should I have moved away from here a long time ago? Other people are leaving their houses and I nod to the woman whose boyfriend seemed to have disappeared a few months back. He's probably back in prison. And didn't she used to be much thinner?

At the station I swipe my card, walk down the escalator, then run and jump into a carriage as the door-closing beeps sound. The train pulls away and I sit down and glance along at the other commuters reading their newspapers and fiddling with their phones. Soon I won't be one of them and this makes me feel a little sick in the stomach.

Staring out through the carriage window opposite, I remember how, when I was very young and travelling with my mother on the tube, I used to kneel on the seat for whole journeys, staring at the dirty thick cables bouncing past on the wall outside.

I pull my phone out of my pocket and thumb through the calendar to find the July 4th page. *7pm – La Memoire*. Isn't that American Independence day?

How many people might turn up? I suppose they'll expect me to stand up and make some sort of a speech, say a few words. 'Good riddance' won't do. Something about how nice they've all been and how I'll miss them. Maybe something funny, to show that I'm not upset about it at all - that I don't care one way or the other.

The train pulls into the station. This is my stop. People are standing up and leaving the carriage and I join them.

'Bomb Walk' previously appeared in *Litro Magazine*; 'Getting On' in *The Whistling Fire*; 'Station' in *Fox Chase Review*; 'Wee Willie Harris' in *Anderbo*; 'Stockwell Road Shots' in *Word Riot*; 'Fitzrovia Junctures' and 'Voyage' in *Stepaway Magazine*.

Printed in Poland
by Amazon Fulfillment
Poland Sp. z o.o., Wrocław